2. noted

THE COLONIAL WARS

1689–1762

The Colonia

THE CHICAGO HISTORY OF AMERICAN CIVILIZATION

Daniel J. Boorstin, EDITOR

Wars 1689-1762

By Howard H. Peckham

THE UNIVERSITY OF CHICAGO PRESS

CHICAGO AND LONDON

THE UNIVERSITY OF CHICAGO PRESS, CHICAGO 60637
THE UNIVERSITY OF CHICAGO PRESS, LTD., LONDON
Published 1964
Printed in the United States of America

02 01 00 99 98 97 96 95 94 93   10 11 12 13 14

ISBN: 0-226-65314-5 (paperbound)

♾ The paper used in this publication meets the minimum requirements of
the American National Standard for Information Sciences—Permanence of
Paper for Printed Library Materials, ANSI Z39.48-1984.

for

DOROTHY

Editor's Preface

The colonial wars which Mr. Peckham recounts in this volume are among the most dramatic and least understood events in our history. They are too often lost in the web of European dynastic conflict, or overshadowed by the momentous war of the Revolution. Yet for American colonists in the seventeenth or eighteenth century they meant life or death. From a European capital the backwoods battles might have seemed only episodes in a continuing, far-flung struggle for empire. But the American remained at the scene of battle. Long after the bands of European soldiers had dissolved or returned across the Atlantic, he reaped a deadly harvest. Each battle left a legacy of new problems which were not solved by the treaties among European powers or settled even by the winning of American independence.

The disproportion between the numbers of men involved and the extent of the consequences was never greater. "On the obscure strife where men died by tens or by scores," wrote Parkman, "hung questions of as deep import for posterity as on those mighty contests of national adolescence where carnage is reckoned by thousands." Since Parkman wrote these words in the year of Appomattox, historians have chosen to give their attention to engagements which were larger, but often much less consequential. Few momentous episodes in our history have been so sparsely chronicled as the history of the colonial wars.

The bright light which historians have fixed on the war of the Revolution has only thrown into deeper shadow the series of wars which preceded it. By 1785 the surviving veterans of '45 were old men. People had found new heroes for the new nation. Names like Sir William Phips, Colonel Benjamin Church, Sir William Pepperrell, and others that had become household words through the struggles which Mr. Peckham recounts in this book suddenly lost their luster. Yet these men too had helped prepare the way for American independence. National heroes who had actually done their part in the French and Indian War—George Washington, Benjamin Franklin, Israel Putnam, and others—were later remembered primarily, or even exclusively, as patriots of the Revolution.

In this volume Mr. Peckham serves all students of American history by illuminating again the actors and the scenes of those colonial wars. He draws together the numerous struggles into a coherent and suspenseful narrative. He shows their relations to one another, and to that continuing struggle for dominance of the New World in which the American Revolution itself was only another beginning. He also observes the distinctive characteristics of warfare in those days. He is at home among

Editor's Preface

both settlers and soldiers, and he takes us with him. In all these ways he serves the purposes of our series.

The "Chicago History of American Civilization" aims to make each aspect of our culture a window to all our history. The series contains two kinds of books: a chronological group, which provides a coherent narrative of American history from its beginning to the present day, and a topical group, which deals with the history of varied and significant aspects of American life. This book is one of the topical group. Twenty-odd titles in the series are in preparation; those already published are listed at the end of this volume. Other episodes in American military history are treated in Mr. Peckham's *War for Independence*, in Otis Singletary's *Mexican War*, and still others will be dealt with in additional volumes now being written.

DANIEL J. BOORSTIN

Table of Contents

Illustrations

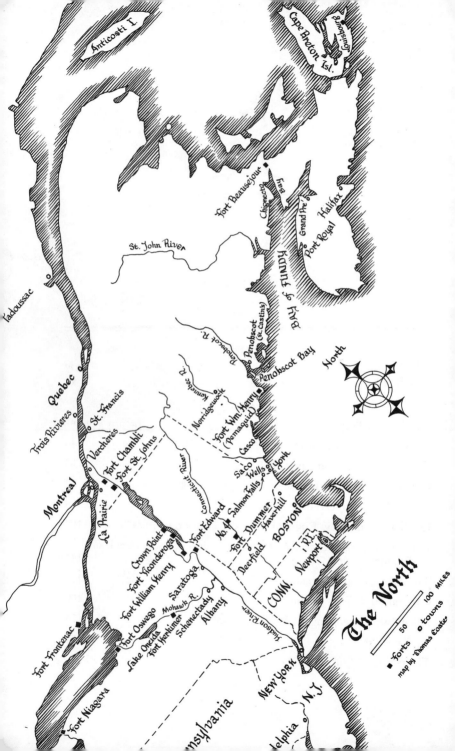

Introduction

central idea derived from intro

American military history began with defenses against Indian attack. It need not be argued here how responsible the whites were for inciting the Indians. The point to be emphasized is that the military experience of early Anglo-Americans was limited to frontier defense for more than eighty years—from 1607 to 1689. *thesis?*

During this same period Europe was torn by the devastating Thirty Years' War (1618–48). Subsequently France fought Spain and Holland, Sweden fought Poland, Germany and Venice fought the Turks, and England, after emerging from civil war, fought Holland twice and Spain once. The French, English, and Spanish who had migrated to the New World escaped all this destruction as well as its education in arms. No military tradition took root in the colonies.

When wars for empire developed among the three colonizing powers their colonies became embroiled. The fighting in

The Colonial Wars

North America between whites, however, differed from European conflicts in at least four particulars. Primitive Indians were enlisted as auxiliary forces or as independent raiders by all three parties. Battles were fought mainly in the wilderness rather than on well-trampled plains; geography prevented the use of cavalry and except in rare instances eliminated sieges of fortified towns. Supplies were always a major problem because the troops were out on the fringes of settlement, far from towns and farms or good roads. Finally, under these different circumstances and from the lack of professional armies, the body of rules generally accepted in Europe was largely ignored. Although discipline was more slack, warfare was more cruel. Prisoners could not be accorded the treatment given them in Europe, the Indians were accustomed to butchering the wounded and plundering, and hospitals were crudely improvised if they were established at all.

In scale the four colonial wars were small operations, of course, until the latter part of the French and Indian War. In the first war, no more than 2,000 men were under arms at one time on any side. This total increased to 5,000 in 1712 when England sent a futile expedition against Quebec. The third war was a smaller affair in general. Not until 1758 did Pitt raise 25,000 troops for service in America—a figure still only one-quarter of France's standing army seventy years earlier.

Casualties were relatively light in battle, ordinarily running less than 10 per cent of the forces engaged, except in such debacles as Wentworth's defeat at Cartagena in 1741 (about 55 per cent) and Braddock's defeat in Pennsylvania in 1755 (69 per cent). Raids on settlements produced higher casualty counts, of course. The combination of poor diet, lack of sanitation, and limited medical knowledge encouraged fatal epi-

2

demics in camp that sometimes carried off more soldiers than fell in battle, as at Louisbourg in 1746 and at Oswego in 1756.

The colonial wars have been suffused by antiquarianism—of the worst and best kind. While some New Englanders devoted themselves to expanding trivial details of only local interest, a few have clarified our knowledge of major issues and campaigns. Foremost was Francis Parkman, who in nine volumes served as a colorful guide through the early wilderness. Occasionally his search for heroes and villains oversimplified or biased his narrative. Today his series of books seems too rich for consumption, while American history textbooks slide rapidly over the whole colonial period before 1763. After all, the colonial wars form the background of less than thirteen of our fifty states. If few Americans can recognize more than Bunker Hill, Valley Forge, and Yorktown in the campaigns of the American Revolution, fewer still can identify Ticonderoga, the Plains of Abraham, or Braddock's defeat in the earlier war, and behind that conflict all is blank. Who now speaks of Louisbourg or Deerfield or Port Royal?

From this distance in time, the several wars appear to be an appalling tale of suffering and unnecessary death, a succession of convulsions that brought no peace until the fourth and final one. The ambitions of essentially little men in Europe could not be satisfied without slaughter, bereavement, and hardship in America in a vain attempt to draw boundaries here that were finally eradicated. Acts of heroism and flashes of glory in these early wars were to be overshadowed by the momentous events of the American Revolution which deadened the echo of earlier drums.

What the Anglo-Americans learned from the colonial wars they translated into political philosophy that led to independence and self-government and to a solution of empire problems through the Ordinance of 1787. This, not conquest, revealed the American genius. Expansion westward was achieved in part by purchase (Louisiana and Florida) and in part by war (against British Canada and the Indians). The challenge of developing a continent made army life, in fact, an unattractive career. Advancement in military science as an end in itself carried no appeal to Americans, although they retained an amateur's receptivity to new tactics and organization and weapons, untempered by the heat of tradition. Disdain for discipline and for training in arms, as well as lack of enough professional officers permitted conquest of only so weak an enemy as Mexico in 1848. Continuation of this military indifference made our Civil War, when it came, long and bloody. Enthusiasm and individual valor were enough to produce casualties, but not enough for either side to win until General Grant applied professional pressure. For long afterward the nation was sick of war. Lack of required military training distinguished us from several European countries. The citizen in arms remained our hero, learning the business of war as he went along. Until 1945 he has always had time.

no unified large army until 1945 there were citizen in arms

I

Europeans vs. Indians

It was inevitable that the American colonies of the several European powers should become involved in the wars of their rival parent countries. The latter were the Atlantic and North Sea nations that had risen to prominence after the discovery of an all-water route to the fabled East. The Mediterranean then lost its place as the center of commerce, and the Italian city-states their eminence in the carrying trade. European eyes turned outward to the vast expanse of the unknown Atlantic Ocean.

EUROPEANS

Little Portugal had found the way around Africa to the East and later settled on the shoulder of South America called Brazil. First to colonize in the New World, however, was Spain, following the discoveries of Columbus. Spreading herself broadly, if thinly, across the West Indies into Mexico and South America, Spain enjoyed the first fruits of foreign riches. Her period of glory was the sixteenth century, when she exploited the Americas, absorbed Portugal, and dominated Europe. Her foreign policy was the most expensive in the world, and not long after the destruction of the armada she sent against England in 1588, her fortunes began to decline.

Shipments of gold and silver bullion fell off as the mines of America approached exhaustion and as smuggling and piracy took their tolls. Spain's population diminished as the colonies attracted the more vigorous Spaniards to emigrate and as hundreds of thousands of Moriscos were expelled for religious reasons. Then came a succession of wars and military defeats in the first half of the seventeenth century by which Spain lost her holdings in the prosperous Netherland provinces and in Italy, failed to hold Portugal, and agreed to make the Pyrenees her boundary with France. By 1660 Spain was finished as a great power in Europe; still she held a vast colonial empire in her somnolent grasp and dreamed of a glorious military past.

When colonization of America began, Spain had the finest army in the world. It drew on the best elements of the population, since Spanish gentlemen considered any profession but arms degrading. Generations had been brought up on tales of battle with the Moors, and with the Reformation a new heretic appeared as enemy. The rigorous Spanish climate produced hardy young men who could endure much; and because a soldier was a person of distinction, the discipline and training that made him efficient were bearable. Merchant seamen provided the base for a navy on which Philip II spent another fortune enlarging.

The army organization of the early 1500's did not change

until after the Spaniards were defeated by the French in 1643. The infantry was formed by *tercios* of three thousand men each, half of them armed with pikes, a third of them with swords and javelins, and the remainder with arquebuses (heavy muskets used with gun rests). In battle the pikemen formed squares, with the swordsmen in their center. The arquebusiers and artillery were drawn up between the squares. Cavalry was a minor arm. Increased use of firearms gradually altered these formations.

In the area of the United States, Spain penetrated the Southwest from Mexico first and the Southeast later, in 1565 founding St. Augustine in Florida. A century later, in 1672, a great stone fort was started there. In addition to the troops already posted in Cuba, Mexico, and Peru, two companies of regulars, amounting to two hundred and eighty officers and men, were dispatched for garrison duty in Florida. Small detachments were stationed in Guale on the Savannah River, at Timucua to the south, and at Apalachee to the west of St. Augustine. In 1688 the regulars totaled three hundred and fifty-five, in three companies. Two companies of militia—one of them free men of color—were formed from the perhaps twelve hundred local inhabitants.

St. Augustine was strictly a military town, a *presidio.* Its economy revolved around the needs of the garrison and the soldiers' pay. And the soldiers were there for two reasons: to guard the Gulf Stream passage of Spanish ships north and south between the mainland and the Bahamas, and to protect the forty to seventy Catholic missionary priests working among the Indians. Political and military power was concentrated in the hands of a governor, who was responsible to the governor of Cuba. He had two civil aides—an accountant and a treasurer

—and a sergeant major as second-in-command of the garrison. These officials, plus a few others, including clerics, composed a *junta*, or temporary council, like the official *cabildo* in other colonies. The junta was an unauthorized advisory body which the governor could call together whenever he wanted help or to share responsibility. Since it was dissolved after each meeting, it carried no interim responsibilities. Regardless of its organization, St. Augustine never prospered, few settlers came, and the colony had to be constantly subsidized.

France had responded slowly to Cartier's early voyage into the St. Lawrence River and grudgingly allowed Samuel de Champlain to establish a colony at Port Royal, Acadia, in 1605, and one at Quebec in 1608. He went on to build a temporary fur post at Montreal in 1611. Until shortly before these events, France had been torn by factions and civil war, achieving unity by wise toleration. Although she was soon to be involved in the Thirty Years' War in Europe, she gathered internal strength after 1663 under the tax reforms of Controller Colbert, who proceeded also to build up the French navy and merchant marine and to encourage colonial trading companies.

From 1666 to 1691 Louis XIV had another exceptionally able minister in the Marquis de Louvois. He reorganized the army and made it the new model for all Europe to emulate. He hurried the replacement of pikes and bows by muskets, to which he attached bayonets. He introduced training for the men, marching in step, uniforms, and regular pay. Louvois insisted that officers tend to their duties, added lieutenant colonels to check on noble colonels and lieutenants to assist noble captains, and appointed inspectors to see that the standards he set were maintained. General officers above colonels were ranked to regularize the flow of authority downward from the king, who was

8

commander in chief. Staffs were provided to plan campaigns. The artillery was attached to the army, and an engineering corps was created.

Louvois built barracks to end the billeting of soldiers in private houses and provided a retirement home for old and disabled veterans. The immensely improved efficiency of the French army was tested and hardened under two great generals of the period, Turenne and Condé. At the same time, an imaginative military engineer, the Marquis de Vauban, devised a successful method of conducting sieges and also fortified French cities against such operations—until it was said that a Vauban city could be taken by no one, except Vauban. Thus it was that by 1689 France had a reputation for invincible arms, and its professional army of one hundred thousand men was both the pride of Louis and the terror of all Europe. It was also enormously expensive.

For all the dominating size of the French army, Louis spared little of it for service in Canada. Never did he send as many as two thousand troops to defend his colony or to capture any of the British colonies. Canada was regarded as the warehouse of a commercial company interested in the fur trade. Failure of the company to provide for the security or well-being of the colony forced Louis to take it over as a royal province in 1662. Immediately he sent over one company of regulars to maintain order, and the first governor he appointed brought a reinforcement. The whole French population in Canada at this time amounted to only three thousand. In 1665 Louis sent over the rest of the Carignan Regiment (twenty-four companies of fifteen hundred men) under Colonel de Salières. It was split up: a garrison protected Quebec; five companies under Captain Sorel built and garrisoned a fort named for him near the

9

mouth of the Richelieu River; others under Captain de Chambly built a second fort farther up the river; a third fort, Ste. Thérèse, was erected almost at its source, which is Lake Champlain; and a fourth, Fort Ste. Anne, was constructed on Île La Motte in the northern part of the lake. These four forts along the favorite Iroquoian route to Montreal were designed for defense. Governor de Tracy sent his regulars and militia against the Mohawks in 1666 and burned their villages. They sued for peace, and in the next year all but four companies of the Carignan Regiment were ordered back to France.

Seigniories were offered to officers of the recalled companies if they would remain as settlers. The grants were large enough that those who took them could sublet tracts to noncommissioned officers and soldiers. The royal treasury also gave them cash to get a feudal colony started around Montreal. Twenty-five to thirty officers and more than four hundred soldiers remained. Five hundred new settlers came in 1670, and six more companies of the Carignan Regiment were returned. The ten companies were now transferred to the Department of the Marine and Colonies and henceforth were known as La Marine Regiment. Early in the 1680's about six hundred more regulars were ordered to Canada as replacements. Governor the Marquis de Denonville was supplied with eight hundred regulars in 1686, which he used, along with a thousand Canadian militia and three hundred Indians, against the Senecas the next year. But when the Indians retaliated and he sought more troops from home, he was advised to make peace!

The province of Canada was ruled by the king, who appointed a governor to act for him in civil and military affairs, and an intendant in charge of financial and judicial matters. If each official was jealous of the other and reported on his rival's actions, so much the better for administration. In addition, the Catholic Church sent over a bishop, and these three officials selected five councilors to serve with them as a governing body. The colonists had little to say and were divided economically into social classes. Grants of land, or seigniories, had been made by the king to favorites. These feudal landowners not only pledged their loyalty to the king but rented land to tenants, milled their wheat for a fee, led them in military service, and acted as their judges. Skilled artisans paid the seignior for the privilege of working at their trades. New settlements were made by granting new seigniories. Many of the Canadians worked in the fur trade, serving the company that held the monopoly or a merchant licensed by the company. They were boatmen and bush rangers. A few attempted private enterprise by pursuing their work independently and illegally, and selling to English traders. These hard, brawling, half-civilized woodsmen had even less interest in self-government than the plodding tenant farmers. What was conspicuously missing was a middle class, large, stable, and flourishing.

England lagged behind France in military prowess. War had become professional in Queen Elizabeth's time, but she would neither pay the expense of a standing army nor employ foreign mercenaries. She placed her reliance on the Royal Navy. England had a kind of militia in "trained bands" in each county serving under a lord lieutenant. Successive kings showed little interest in a professional army until Charles I faced a rebellion in Scotland in 1639 and discovered that the trained bands looted and rioted much better than they fought. Civil war followed, with king and Parliament each raising an army. Out of the contest emerged the New Model Army of 1645 that came under the command of Oliver Cromwell. The men were organized

[handwritten margin notes: "descp. new model Army"; "respected, rules"; "England weak army no respect"]

into regiments of ten companies each. Scarlet uniforms were adopted. Pay remained at eight pence a day, most of it withheld or "stopped" for clothing and food. A Parliamentary committee looked after the men; a treasurer of war handled financial matters; and an office of ordnance supplied weapons and stores.

Upon the restoration of the monarchy in 1660, Charles II identified the army with Parliament's revolt, so he set about reducing it, keeping only a small corps of guards to protect his person. He also reorganized the militia so that the king commanded it. But in three successive wars with the Dutch the army had to be increased. Parliament, however, never recognized its existence and never provided for it. The king paid the costs of the army himself, sometimes using money voted for the militia, sometimes selling commissions. Another way was to borrow money secretly from Louis XIV, who harbored the remote hope of restoring Catholicism in England. There was no military law: disobedient soldiers had to be tried in civil courts, and some infractions such as desertion or sleeping on duty were not civil offenses and could not be punished. Military service carried little prestige. The officer corps was a not too demanding profession for young noblemen, and the ranks were the last refuge of desperate men.

From the homeland, then, the English colonies could not expect much military aid. In fact, England had left to stock companies the sponsorship of settlements in Virginia in 1607 and Plymouth in 1620, and to proprietors the attracting of settlers to the Jersies, Pennsylvania, Maryland, Delaware, and Carolina. Charles I had involved England in a brief war with France in 1628 and casually allowed the three Kirke brothers to lead a squadron that captured both Port Royal and Quebec. The French posts were restored at the peace table.

By the end of the century stock companies and proprietors had been disappointed, and most of the English colonies were under royal supervision. The king appointed the governor, but the colony was ruled, in contrast to a Spanish or French colony, by an assembly of two houses modeled after Parliament. The upper chamber or council, appointed by the Crown, in addition to its legislative function formed the highest court in the colony. The lower house was made up of representatives elected by free adult males who possessed some property. They held the purse strings, even on the governor's salary, and frequently were at odds with the governor and council. The laws they enacted could be disallowed by the Privy Council. Local or county courts with elected judges were provided throughout each colony. Town meetings in New England elected local officials and passed ordinances, while in the South the church vestrymen served the civil interests of their parish. Self-government to this extent was firmly embedded and zealously guarded by this middle-class society. Connecticut and Rhode Island were special situations, so democratic as to elect their governors and legislatures; the king permitted this freedom so long as their laws were in harmony with England's.

The Dutch, who had penetrated both East and West Indies, found the Hudson River and staked out a fur-trading post in 1614 near Albany, later building Fort Orange. In 1625 a Dutch colony settled on Manhattan Island and developed New Amsterdam. Then the Swedes appeared on the Delaware River, an area claimed by the Dutch. The Dutch seized the Swedish settlements and by 1655 had eliminated them from America. England in turn grew irritated at seeing Dutch expansion between the two developing English zones and boldly captured New Amsterdam in 1664, renaming it New York. In a second Dutch war, France joined Holland during the last few months of 1667, thereby spurring Holland as well as England to make peace. Nothing in this war happened in America except that the French marched on the troublesome Mohawks, and the governor of New York tried without success to arouse New England to join him in attacking Montreal and Quebec.

Above Quebec the frozen North lay open to the French until 1670, when by an astute move the British established a post in Hudson Bay. Thus Canada found itself hemmed in north and south, but with the vast interior of the continent wide open. Possessing the only water routes into the West, the French paddled up the St. Lawrence and Ottawa rivers to the Great Lakes. Forts appeared at both ends of Lake Ontario, and St. Ignace on the Straits of Mackinac controlled the upper trade route. Dauntless explorers discovered the great Mississippi River and ventured into the Illinois country. La Salle even planned a post at the mouth of the mighty river, but lost his life in a futile effort to locate it. English colonies might claim a long Atlantic coast line, but they had no depth, and France was determined that they should remain on the Appalachian shelf.

To the south, Virginians had pushed down into modern North Carolina, but Charleston harbor was settled by aggressive Englishmen from Barbados in 1670. They promptly attacked St. Augustine but were driven off, and Spain began its fortification. The Spaniards looked upon the Charlestonians as invaders anyway, and in 1686 the governor sent an expedition northward. Although it wiped out a four-year-old Scot settlement on Port Royal Island, a hurricane saved Charleston from assault.

In the third Anglo-Dutch war, the Dutch recaptured New York but gave it up in the peace treaty of 1674. To safeguard it in the future, England recruited an Independent Company and dispatched it with Governor Edmund Andros to receive the colony back from the Dutch. The company consisted of a hundred privates, two drummers, six noncommissioned officers, an ensign, and two lieutenants. After arrival it was divided for duty between Albany and New York City. These were the first British "regulars" to be stationed in America.

Two years later a battalion of five companies, each two hundred strong, was sent to Virginia under Colonel Herbert Jeffreys in the wake of Bacon's rebellion against the royal governor. Four of the companies were returned home in 1678, but another was sent over so that Virginia had two companies until 1682, when both were disbanded because the Virginia House of Burgesses refused to support them.

Late in 1686, when Andros became governor of the Dominion of New England, he brought in two more Independent Companies, of fifty privates each. Two years later New York and New Jersey were added to the Dominion, and the old first company was split into two. There were then four Independent Companies, totaling two hundred men plus their officers.

It was clear by this time that colony planting was far from a peaceful business. Two European powers had been eliminated from American shores by force. The other three had already exchanged blows in North America. All were governed from home, but received little military aid. The three nationalities were arranged in sandwich layers from north to south down the Atlantic coast: English, French, English, Spanish. They were expected by their own exertions to subdue nature, to determine their own boundaries by force against or by settlement with their rivals, and also to face the native inhabitants, the Indians. It was, indeed, these fourth parties who shaped and sharpened the national hostilities in America. They references

12

were sought as pagans to Christianize, as workers to produce furs or corn or minerals, and as warriors to augment military forces. They were also regarded as barriers to expansion and as a menace to peaceful existence. Each of the European rivals created its own disciples and devils among the redskinned natives.

INDIANS

When settlement began, the Europeans were as ignorant of how to treat the aborigines as they were of how to survive in the wilderness. They learned the woodsman's arts in the harsh school of experience. They never learned to keep the peace with the Indians. For their own purposes were full of unresolvable conflicts.

The Indians did not present a united front to the white man. They were divided into warring tribes of varying cultural levels who spoke a bewildering variety of languages and did not appear to be permanently domiciled in any one spot. Although the Indians vastly improved and enlarged the European's meager diet and introduced him to the bark canoe, the moccasin and snowshoe, and tobacco, they aroused his cupidity by their obvious needs and their complete ignorance of private property in land and minerals. In warfare they were astoundingly capable and tireless scouts, fierce fighters in surprise attacks, and barbaric in their treatment of prisoners. But they had no patience or supplies for sieges.

In Florida the Spaniards encountered four major tribes or confederations of the Muskhogean language group: the savage Caloosans and Tequestas who divided the lower half of the peninsula, the Timucuas in the northern half, and the Apalachees to the west. These tribes may have totaled twenty thousand.

Europeans vs. Indians

Spanish policy was paternalistic, and missions were a prime interest because the Indians were viewed as a labor supply, and conversion made them more tractable. The Jesuits gave up the job as hopeless, but some Franciscans persevered and gradually a few mission stations were set up to the west; yet only St. Augustine could be called a town. Not self-supporting, Florida represented a weak extension of the Spanish Empire, and though it never threatened the Indians with crowding, it did demand their submission or removal.

Farther north the initial reception of English and French colonists was more hospitable, but there were native complications prophetic of trouble. In the midst of the Algonquin-speaking tribes of northeastern North America lived an island of Iroquois in central New York State and on either side of Lake Erie. For reasons lost in antiquity these two groups of tribes were hostile in 1600. From the map, it might seem that the surrounded Iroquois were at a decided disadvantage, but as the seventeenth century unrolled, the Iroquois developed into the scourge of their divided neighbors. To a great natural ferocity they added the strength of organization by uniting the Mohawks, Oneidas, Onondagas, Cayugas, and Senecas. From this "defensive" league of perhaps twelve thousand, the Eries on the south side of Lake Erie and the Hurons on the north side were excluded, or they refused to join. As a result the Eries were exterminated in the 1650's, and the Hurons were reduced and forced to associate themselves with Algonquin tribes farther west. The Susquehannas to the south were reduced to a satellite, and dominion over the Lenapé, or Delawares, of eastern Pennsylvania was claimed.

It was the luck of Champlain to establish the French on the St. Lawrence among the Algonquins. They had but recently been attacked by the Iroquois and, when they beheld firearms for the first time, they urged these strange and powerful white warriors to join them in a raid on their enemies. Champlain acquiesced, and in the fall of 1609 took two soldiers on an expedition southwestward to the lake that bears his name. There, in a brief battle that colored the whole course of empire, the French won a victory over the Iroquois that plagued them for a hundred and fifty years.

The Iroquois learned quickly and brutally. Soon getting muskets from the Dutch, they practiced on their neighbors and joined with any white allies who were willing to fight the French or their Algonquin allies. Only a few French Jesuits penetrated this spruce curtain. They weakened the Iroquois a little by drawing off some converts to a Christian village near Montreal. Farther east the French held sway over the Abenakis of modern Maine, the Montagnais north of them, and the Micmacs of Nova Scotia and the islands. In the West the French gradually drew into their economic orbit the Algonquins of the Great Lakes: Ottawa, Chippewa, Potawatomi, Miami, Sauk, and Fox.

Around Jamestown, in Virginia, the English found other groups of Algonquin tribes who alternately fed and feuded with them. The threat of newcomers did not seem formidable to the Powhatan confederation for the first fifteen years, because in that period although about ten thousand Englishmen came to Virginia (some returning home) and produced children, only about twelve hundred were alive in 1622. In that year hostility over land acquisition culminated in a surprise attack that killed almost a third of the settlers. The tragedy inspired a vengeance that exterminated enough Indians to keep them quiet for two decades. But in 1644 they rose again and killed more than three hundred whites. This time the Indians were driven back from the tidewater area.

In New England the Pilgrims, who wanted nothing so much as to be left alone, found an uninhabited patch of ground at Plymouth in 1620 and became good neighbors to the Wampanoags. On the other hand, the Puritans at Boston ten years later, enjoying the delusion of being a Chosen People entering a new Canaan and misconceiving the scriptural responsibilities of such a role, were not long in discerning the Indians to be Canaanites (on whom the Old Testament wasted no sympathy) or minions of a very real Devil. Missionary activity in general suffered Calvinistic neglect, and the pagans' resistance to selling their lands was not taken seriously. Friction developed rapidly, and a flame was first ignited in the distant Connecticut River valley where the expanding English had planted a new settlement. The local Pequots resented the trespass and killed nine of the new arrivals. Massachusetts Bay retaliated with troops in 1637 who killed several hundred Pequots and drove the survivors into neighboring tribes.

The St. Lawrence Algonquins clung to the French for life, while the Great Lakes tribes were exposed to terror raids by the Iroquois for the offense of trading with the French. Ultimately the Indians of Pennsylvania and Virginia felt the bullets and tomahawks of the Iroquois even as they fell back before the encroachment of the whites. The Indians of Long Island and the lower Hudson were the victims of aggressive Dutch burghers before New Netherland passed to the English Crown. Now Englishmen at Albany became the brethren of the Iroquois and heartily encouraged their ancient enmity toward the French.

The Delawares, who had greeted the Dutch and Swedes

along the river of their name, were well treated when William Penn met them in 1682. Farther south, below Virginia, the later English settlers had encountered principally the Tuscarora, Cherokee, Catawba, Yamasee, and the Creek confederation. All of them were more agricultural than the northern tribes. The Tuscaroras were a detached Iroquoian-speaking group in North Carolina and, like their New York cousins, found the white man irritating. They were to give serious trouble later. The Cherokees in the same region farther west were a huge tribe generally friendly to the English until 1759. The Catawbas in the South Carolina back country did not feel crowded by the coastal plantations. The great Creek nation was built around a dominant group of Muskogees and extended from Georgia's coast to central Alabama. Their general hostility toward the Florida tribes caused them to be friendly to the Spanish-hating English. Wedged against the Creeks were the Yamasees, who first inhabited northern Florida but, after some trouble with the Spaniards in 1685, moved up to the Savannah River. They would rise against the English in 1715.

Up in New England the situation grew more explosive. There the tribes found themselves between the English hammer and the Iroquoian anvil. Growth of the white population led to an uprising of Wampanoags, Nipmucks, and Narragansetts under Chief Metacomet, or "King Philip," in 1675. Towns throughout southern New England suffered, but the weight of the white numbers soon told. Philip was killed, and with him died tribal life and the fur trade in this area. New England had only a northern frontier to guard against the French and their Indian allies. The Iroquois alone could be counted as effective friends, and they were not steadfast because of their deeply felt independence.

Europeans vs. Indians

To the pivotal colony of New York came Colonel Thomas Dongan as governor in 1683. Although appointed by a Catholic king who was secretly receiving a pension from Louis XIV, Dongan was thoroughly British and suspicious of the French. When he perceived that the westward thrust of the French was turning southward, he grew apprehensive. Catholic though he was, he set himself to stopping French expansion and even asserted that New York's northern boundary was the St. Lawrence River. He was anxious to develop English trade with the western tribes that France was bringing under her aegis. The immediate situation gave him an opportunity, for the Iroquois had launched war on the distant Illinois confederation, forcing the French to go to their aid by striking at the Iroquois towns.

Dongan countered with an offer to help defend the Iroquois if they would acknowledge themselves to be under English jurisdiction. The Iroquois accepted the proposal, and Dongan notified Governor Denonville that he must cease annoying the Iroquois because they were British subjects. The Canadian governor denied this startling claim, as he had denied the New York boundary, and led French troops and numerous Indian allies to attack the Senecas in 1687. He burned five towns and their crops, then moved over to Niagara to rebuild the old French fort. In reprisal the Iroquois, supplied with powder and arms by the New York governor, laid siege to Montreal the next year. Denonville appealed to Dongan to call off his Indian subjects, but Dongan proposed unacceptable conditions.

To consolidate administration of his colonies, King James recalled Dongan and named the autocratic Sir Edmund Andros to be governor of a new Dominion consisting of New York and New Jersey added to New England. The Iroquois, disgruntled at obtaining no further help from the English, returned to their villages, but they were not through with the French.

In exerting his personal authority, Governor Andros, with the soldiers he had brought over, seized the trading post of Baron de St. Castin on remote Penobscot Bay. St. Castin was an army officer who had been discharged in Canada and who had obtained a grant of land at Penobscot and taken an Indian wife. He was allowed to retire into the woods. The French then incited the Abenakis of Maine to ravage the northern frontier and in August, 1689, to destroy the rival English post at Pemaquid (Bristol, Maine), fifty miles closer to Boston.

Meanwhile, Europe had once again descended into war. Louis XIV declared war on Hapsburg Austria in September, 1688, to gain a Rhine frontier. At the same time in England the Catholic and Francophile James II was driven from the throne, and in November Parliament called his Protestant daughter Mary and her husband, Prince William of Orange, to be joint monarchs. In accepting, they acknowledged the superior authority of Parliament and laid to rest any lingering notions about the divine right of kings. They also agreed to a Bill of Rights alleviating specific grievances of the people. This change upset the British army. One regiment stayed loyal to James and mutinied. Thereupon Parliament passed a Mutiny Act, providing for courts-martial and military law for six months. One item in the Bill of Rights prohibited the new monarchs from keeping a standing army in time of peace without the consent of Parliament. The king might choose its officers, but Parliament would pay the army one year at a time, just as it would renew the Mutiny Act annually. Thus if the king did not call Parliament each year and submit his requests, the army would fall apart for lack of pay and discipline. This was England's check on ambitious monarchs and her feeble answer to Louis' immense standing army.

When news reached America of this "Glorious Revolution," the reactionary Governor Andros was overthrown in April, 1689, while Massachusetts and New York seized as king's men the hapless officers of the four Independent Companies. The military units simply dissolved. The cumbersome Dominion fell apart, and in New York a popular leader named Jacob Leisler grabbed control, designating himself as lieutenant governor until the new monarchs should act. Albany, its two thousand inhabitants scattered in county and town and still predominantly Dutch, refused to recognize Leisler and governed itself through a mayor and council.

The Austrian emperor, who had won Sweden and Spain to his side, signed a treaty with Holland in May, 1689, to which Dutch William attached England. Hence they all entered the war against France. Louis' diplomacy had failed to avert an alliance against him.

In July the relentless and single-minded Iroquois attacked Lachine, six miles from Montreal, and perpetrated the worst massacre in all Canadian history. Although one estimate is that sixty-six French were killed, Governor Denonville reported the number at two hundred, with more than a hundred taken prisoner. In fright the governor recalled the garrisons from Fort Niagara and Fort Frontenac to strengthen Montreal.

When official war came at last, both English and French in America were counting heavily on Indian allies and calculating sharply the impact of Indian enemies. The pattern was irregular and complex. The French felt sure of the loyalty of the tribes along the St. Lawrence, especially the alleged Christian ones at Caughnawaga and St. Francis, and those to the east and south. But to hold the loyalty of the tribes of the western Great Lakes and upper Mississippi would require fair treatment by traders and soldiers, gifts from government, suppression of Iroquois raids, and above all a victory or two by the French to demonstrate their superiority.

The English were confident at the moment of help in New York from the Iroquois, but New England lay open. South of them were friendly tribes that would not be active as long as the war did not touch them. Neutrality was the best that could be expected. Although Spain was on England's side, no help was anticipated from Florida because it had no French neighbors.

II

Militia at the Frontiers
King William's War

When news reached the English colonies during the summer of 1689 that Britain had declared war on France, Massachusetts and New York had already exchanged blows with their popish neighbors to the north. Yet these forays had been localized hostilities, like fights between neighboring children, which the parent countries could smooth over. This time, however, the parents were fully committed. The enemy was common on both sides of the Atlantic for both Englishman and Frenchman.

Europeans called it the War of the League of Augsburg, and long afterward some historians referred to it as the beginning of a new Hundred Years' War in Europe, ending at Waterloo in 1815—actually a hundred and twenty-five years. Americans, looking back and remembering that it occurred in the new king's reign, called it King William's War. More accurately it was the first of four French and Indian wars. It lasted eight years.

As a measure of self-protection, the English colonists had organized a militia that included every able-bodied man from sixteen to sixty. The Puritans of New England were a committed people, ever ready to defend themselves and their religion by force of arms if necessary. As early as 1638 the Ancient and Honorable Artillery Company had been organized in Boston to study gunnery. The preamble to the Massachusetts Bay militia law of 1643 stated, "as piety cannot be maintained without church ordinances & officers, nor justice without lawes & magistracy, no more can our safety & peace be preserved without military orders & officers." Exempt from service were ministers, magistrates, physicians, schoolmasters, fishermen, and Harvard students, but other men were to turn out four to six days a year for inspection and training. The other colonies enacted similar laws. At first, one-third of the militia was equipped as pikemen, and two-thirds as musketeers. The former being found useless in the woods, all became musketeers equipped with sure-fire matchlocks, replaced by flintlocks by 1675. Carbines and pistols were also used. Each town was required to have a band or company, and those men who could afford to furnish horses were organized into troopers or cavalry. Usually each company elected its own officers, although the governor was commander in chief. Only Pennsylvania had no militia system. The professional companies from England, unknown before 1674, had again disappeared. Now in this first joint war effort, the American amateurs, experienced principally in Indian conflict, would be tested.

Canadians were similarly organized in provincial militia. Un-

26

der the seigniorial system, military service was a duty that the tenants owed the landowners, and the landowners owed the king, a feudal concept. Since it was a familiar condition of colonial life, there was little objection to it. In each parish an appointed captain led his militia company; in time of action companies were organized into battalions and field officers appointed. As regulars, Canada had the various companies of La Marine Regiment. Its strength fluctuated between five hundred and perhaps twelve hundred men, frequently composed of recruits of the poorest sort shipped over from France. The Canadian government could also marshal Indian allies and call on missionaries or *coureurs de bois* (fur traders and adventurers in the forest) to lead them. No prime French regulars were available to Canada.

BOLDNESS ON BOTH SIDES

Since the Iroquois had delivered a staggering blow to Canada with impunity and forced the French to relax their hold on Lake Ontario, the next move was clearly up to the Canadian government. Louis had recalled Governor Denonville and in desperation summoned the Comte de Frontenac to return to Canada for a second term as governor. He was a professional soldier, having been a brigadier general at the age of twenty-six. First appointed governor of Canada in 1672—possibly because he had become intimate with Louis' favorite mistress— he demonstrated great energy and purpose; but being domineering and ill-tempered, he quarreled with everyone and ten years later was recalled. Now that the perilous situation required boldness and purpose, the king reappointed him in spite of his seventy years. He was authorized to invade and capture the colony of New York at once. Only his delayed arrival—he reached Quebec in October, 1689—prevented the attempt.

The Indian raid on Montreal demanded some sort of military victory, both to cow the Iroquois and to keep the allegiance of the wavering western tribes. Moreover, New York was an inviting target because of its divided political status. During the winter of 1689–90 Frontenac planned three raids to be undertaken by joint forces of Canadian regulars, militia, and Indians. They were to strike at Albany, New Hampshire, and Maine. Hoping at the same time to deceive and neutralize the Iroquois, Frontenac invited them to a peace council in the early spring.

Still managing its own affairs, Albany was fearful but not inactive. It urged the Iroquois not to answer any overtures from the enemy and even held out the hope of driving the French out of Canada altogether—a seemingly impossible and overambitious aim at this time, but one that appealed to the Iroquois. The Albany town council sought reinforcement, not from New York, which would require recognition of Lieutenant Governor Leisler, but from neighboring Connecticut, which responded by sending eighty-seven men to Albany for the winter. Twenty-five were forwarded to the frontier post of Schenectady, fifteen miles northwest of Albany and containing about one hundred and fifty Dutch traders and farmers and their Negro slaves in a stockaded village. (Leisler would later accuse Connecticut of sending its troops solely to support Albany's intransigence.)

In the midst of winter a party of two hundred and ten Canadians and Christianized Indians in about equal numbers set out from Montreal southward under the command of Captain Jacques Le Moyne de Ste. Hélène, of a distinguished Canadian family, and Lieutenant D'Aillebout de Mantet. They slid down over the ice of Lake Champlain and Lake George and then melted into the dark woods. Somewhere along the route the goal was changed from strongly defended Albany to small Schenectady. On the cold and blustery night of February 8, 1690, the expedition approached the sleeping village. Its log houses were enclosed by an oblong stockade of pickets, yet the gates stood open and unguarded except for a pair of snow men! Such neglect is inexplicable.

The Canadians filed into the silent town shortly before midnight and encircled the houses, then fell on the inhabitants indiscriminately. In two hours, sixty were killed, including eleven Negroes, and except for a few who escaped in the darkness the rest were taken prisoner. The settlement was set afire, and sixty-three houses and a Dutch Reformed church were destroyed. Only one Frenchman and one Indian had been killed. When the marauders withdrew, they left behind about sixty old men, women, and children, but carried off twenty-seven captives, including five Negroes. Eleven of these escaped in the next several months.

Albany was aroused and dismayed by the news, and so were the Mohawks, who denounced the perfidy of Frontenac for ordering this attack while trying to talk peace with them. Exposure of the ruse ruined whatever success the governor might have had in neutralizing them. A pursuit party of Albany men and Mohawks followed the raiders northward but could not bring them to battle. Almost within sight of the St. Lawrence shots were exchanged and half a dozen casualties inflicted before the environs of Montreal swallowed the Canadians.

With perception and dispatch the Albany government before the end of the month sent Robert Livingston to New England and another emissary to New York City to ask for

Leisler govt Albany

troops and to urge a sea attack on Quebec. Some of the Albany women and children were moved far down the Hudson. Lieutenant Governor Leisler also appealed to the neighboring colonies for a conference in New York City late in April. He likewise took advantage of Albany's fears to send up one hundred and sixty men under his tool and future son-in-law, Jacob Milborne, ostensibly to reinforce the town. Since Connecticut was demanding return of its troops, the Albany magistrates had no choice but to accept Milborne's help, which meant acknowledging Leisler as the legitimate executive. He had come to New York in 1660 as a soldier for the Dutch West India Company, married well, and became a rich merchant. Ambitious and dictatorial, he had alienated his friends by his obstinate temper and his ruthless imprisonment of any opponents.

Before this political change took place, the French struck again. A party of fifty Canadians and Indians ("half Indianized French, and half Frenchified Indians," according to the Reverend Cotton Mather) under Captain François Hertel de Rouville, once a tortured captive of the Mohawks, swept out of Trois Rivières and on March 18 struck the frontier town of Salmon Falls, New Hampshire, thirteen miles north of Portsmouth. Breaking in on two stockaded places and a fortified house, they killed thirty-four residents and carried off fifty-four. This fresh attack underscored the need for united resistance and overcame the reluctance of the colonies to respond to the invitation of a man whom many regarded as a usurper.

Massachusetts moved independently against its favorite objective: Port Royal in Acadia. Command of an expedition was given to Sir William Phips, forty years old and for Boston a colorful character. Born at Pemaquid, he had found work in the city as a ship carpenter. Here he heard of a sunken Spanish treasure ship off one of the Bahamas. In 1687 he organized a salvaging operation, found the ship, and recovered a fortune in gold, silver, and jewels. Having sailed to England with his treasure, he was knighted by King James II, perhaps for his feat of transporting such a valuable cargo safely across the Atlantic. He returned wealthy and famous to Boston and joined the church of the influential Mathers. His respectability was now unimpeachable.

With seven hundred men Phips sailed north on May 9, 1690, in fourteen ships of various size and entered Port Royal ten days later. The garrison of sixty under Captain Meneval surrendered in hope of saving the town. But Phips believed that certain inhabitants were violating the terms of surrender, and so he allowed his men to desecrate the church and plunder the merchants. The Canadians were forced to take an oath of allegiance to the British Crown, and certain local officials were appointed who were to consider themselves under the jurisdiction of Massachusetts. Phips returned to Boston in triumph, landing his military prisoners, two priests, and various stores on May 30. A few days after his departure from Port Royal, a French ship arrived. Then two pirate ships appeared, captured the French vessel, burned twenty-eight houses, hanged two inhabitants, and plundered the town once more.

While Port Royal was taken out of the war by these double attacks, Governor Frontenac's third stroke was delivered in Maine. A party of fifty Canadians and seventy Abenakis under Captain Portneuf and Lieutenant Courtemanche set out from Quebec. It was joined on the Kennebec River by Captain de Rouville and thirty-six of his party still afield after the raid on Salmon Falls. They were soon augmented by other Indians and Baron de St. Castin to make a task force of about five hundred.

They fell on Casco (Falmouth), May 27, killing twenty inhabitants. The others fled that night to Fort Loyal (Portland) where Captain Sylvanus Davis commanded a small garrison.

The invaders laid siege to the fort, and on the fourth day Davis knew he must give up to the assailing horde. He had supposed that the attackers were all Indians, and perhaps the Canadians were painted and dressed like their allies. In seeking terms, he learned that there were Frenchmen outside. "Upon this answer, we sent out to them again, to know from whence they came, and if they would give us good quarter, both for our men, women, and children, both wounded and sound; and [to demand] that we should have liberty to march to the next English town—then we would surrender; and also that the governour of the French should hold up his hand, and swear by the great and ever-living God, that the several articles should be performed. All which he did solemnly swear to perform."

The gates swung open, and the Americans filed out. Immediately the French allowed the Indians to butcher at will, and about a hundred men, women, and children fell victim to savage fury on the curious ground offered later by the French that they were in rebellion against their lawful king, the deposed James II! The fort was destroyed, and Captain Davis, with three or four others, was carried to Quebec.

The first intercolonial conference convened at New York during the last days of April, 1690, with representatives attending from Massachusetts Bay, Plymouth, Connecticut, and New York. Maryland was represented only by a letter from the governor offering a hundred men to any joint military enterprise. Rhode Island promised money rather than men. Virginia took no part because Francis Nicholson, whom Leisler had forced out of New York, had just been appointed lieutenant governor of that colony, and the House of Burgesses was reluctant to act. Pennsylvania was temporarily without a governor and did not reply. A New England confederation for defense (without Rhode Island) had flourished back in 1643, but after King Philip's War it fell apart. Present plans called for a united invasion of Canada by land and by sea. The several provinces agreed to furnish troops for the overland expedition in the following proportions:

New York	400
Connecticut	135
Massachusetts Bay	160
Plymouth	60
	755
Maryland	100
	855

According to Leisler, the Iroquois talked of contributing eighteen hundred warriors. Although Massachusetts Bay held twice the population of New York, its proffered quota was small because it had already recruited seven hundred men for Port Royal and expected to furnish many more troops and seamen for the seaborne attack on Quebec.

Leisler harbored some hope of leading the overland force against Montreal himself, but with so many political enemies he did not dare leave his state. When he appointed his friend Milborne as commander in chief, the men already under arms and the province of Connecticut objected vigorously. Their choice was Major Fitz-John Winthrop, formerly a British army officer and son of a Connecticut governor. Reluctantly, Leisler gave in at the last moment, and Milborne became commissary, where his incompetence was largely responsible for stopping the expedition.

The Colonial Wars

Leisler was at least energetic: he called his stooge assembly to enact a tax on real and personal property for military purposes and exacted it over the people's protests. He also fitted out three ships to go against Quebec, although they never cooperated with the Massachusetts task force. Instead, they simply cruised and took several French prizes for their own profit.

Perhaps the delegates to the New York conference reviewed the war resources of the two belligerents in America. On paper a decided advantage seemed to lie with the English colonies. They contained a population of about 205,000, almost half of it in New England and New York. Canada could not count more than 13,000, but a large proportion of the population were men, among whom many had seen military service. Further, the Canadians could muster a larger number of Indian allies than the English, and they had already demonstrated raiding tactics along the frontier that were as difficult to parry as they were to prevent.

Both the Anglo-Americans and the Canadians expected help from their mother countries and had dispatched appeals. Canada was the more desperately in need, for it could barely feed itself in peaceful times and certainly could not when men were called from the fields to fight. Response of the parent countries remained to be measured.

The joint expedition against Montreal ended dismally. Massachusetts Bay and Plymouth never sent any men to Albany. None from Maryland appeared. New York managed to raise only one hundred and fifty, and Connecticut alone seems to have filled its quota of one hundred and thirty-five. At Albany in July smallpox broke out before the men marched. The Iroquois also suffered from smallpox and only a few hundred showed up. Although insufficient supplies were on hand when Major Winthrop started his men northward on July 30, delivery was promised by Milborne. The men were moved up to Wood Creek near its juncture with Lake Champlain. There they waited for the Indians to make additional canoes and for provisions to catch up, but it was the wrong season for stripping birch trees and no supplies appeared.

Captain John Schuyler got permission to proceed down the lake with volunteers. He left on August 13 with twenty-nine soldiers and one hundred and twenty Indians. Winthrop waited two days more and held another council with his officers; they decided they could not advance and therefore should return. In a week they were back at Albany. Leisler was infuriated with what he considered Winthrop's cowardice and disobedience and clapped him into jail, until Connecticut soldiers protested so loudly that he was released. Thoroughly antagonized, Connecticut's governor wrote to Leisler: "A prison is not a catholicon for all state maladies, though so much used by you."

Captain Schuyler, only twenty-two and brother of Albany's mayor, met Captain Johannes Glen, who had been spared in the Schenectady massacre, with a party of twenty-eight whites and five Indians. Schuyler enlisted the Indians and thirteen of the soldiers to join his mission. Thus reinforced, the men paddled down the length of Lake Champlain, traveling at night, and entered the Richelieu River. Three miles from Fort Chambly they hid their canoes, and on August 23 turned west and fell on the French settlement of La Prairie, across the St. Lawrence from Montreal. They killed six men, took nineteen prisoners, shot one hundred and fifty head of cattle, and burned sixteen houses, plus barns and haystacks. The Indians would not attack the fort itself, which was firing an alarm gun and

did not attack D

being answered by Montreal. So the expedition turned back. The Indians killed two French prisoners who were wounded and could not keep up. Taking to their canoes, the raiders reached Albany on August 30, having wreaked the only revenge for Schenectady, and no more than that.

Meanwhile, Massachusetts had raised approximately two thousand men and gathered thirty-four ships for the grand naval attack on Quebec. Command of the expedition was given, of course, to the popular and victorious Sir William Phips. The troops were under Major John Walley, formerly a member of the council. The armada sailed on August 21 with provisions for four months—but without a pilot who knew the St. Lawrence River. Partly on that account and partly because of adverse winds, the expedition took an incredible eight weeks to come in sight of the Canadian capital on its rock. The date was October 17, 1690, and the weather already cold.

A haughty bid from Phips to the town to surrender was insolently refused by Governor Frontenac himself. After the threat to Montreal had evaporated, Frontenac had had time to come down with reinforcements, gathering more on the way, so that he now commanded three thousand regulars and militia crowded around Quebec. If Phips wanted the citadel he must either batter it down with his ships' cannon or storm the walls.

The Americans landed more than twelve hundred men on the north shore where the St. Charles River emptied, just east of Quebec. They waded ashore at low tide expecting to march up the tributary until they could cross to the rear of the town but found some six hundred Frenchmen posted in the marshy woods. Six field guns were ferried to them and promptly sank in the soft ground. Persisting, the New Englanders used up most of their ammunition in dislodging the French but could not pursue them. Each man had been furnished with only two biscuits, and these were consumed by the end of the day. When Major Walley sent back to the ships for more ammunition and food, he received only one half-barrel of powder. Then the ships pulled away and began shelling Quebec, without waiting for any co-ordinated advance by the soldiers. The vessels did little damage—twenty livres would pay for all repairs, the French declared—and they were generously shelled in return. Yet the bombardment was resumed next day until two ships were seriously hit.

When the warships again established contact with the landing party on the second night, they sent ashore a "bisket cake" per man. Slightly refreshed, the New Englanders now attempted to cross the St. Charles in an unsupported land offensive but were stalled by the French. Hunger was relieved by butchering some cattle, and on the next day skirmishing continued. Walley went out to the flagship to confer with Phips. Since no more powder was available, the troops were called aboard. Only one cannon was recovered. The fighting had cost thirty killed, according to Phips, and twice as many wounded. About thirty Frenchmen had been killed, including Ste. Hélène, commander of the raid on Schenectady, and seventeen captured. Phips lingered down the river to repair his ships (he himself worked on them) and to arrange an exchange of the prisoners for seventeen Englishmen taken on the frontiers, including Captain Davis of Maine.

Smallpox having made its appearance, the expedition sailed for home. Could it have remained another week, Quebec might have fallen for want of food for its inflated population. Two vessels were cast away, one burned, and two hundred men reportedly perished in these accidents and from disease. Phips himself reached Boston harbor late in November, his other ships straggling in later. Luckily for him the Calvinistic inhabitants blamed the defeat on God rather than on the want of military capacity in Phips when faced with tough opposition. He soon departed for England.

The fruitless expedition cost Massachusetts Bay more than £50,000, which it did not have and hopefully had expected to acquire from loot after Quebec fell. To pay the clamoring soldiers and sailors, it issued paper money and laid heavy taxes to redeem the paper. This was the first issue of paper money in America and in the British Empire, a practice that continued during (and perhaps made possible) the successive French and Indian wars.

Thus ended the first year of the war. If Canada had enjoyed the best of the conflict, she was by her very exertions unable to resume the offensive during the coming winter for want of food, ammunition, and blankets.

THE SECOND ROUND

The military failure in and by New York increased both local dissatisfaction with Lieutenant Governor Leisler's inept autocracy and his own determination to stifle opposition. Instead of growing disturbed and more tractable under the long silence from London about recognizing him, he became more domineering and intolerable. When Major Richard Ingoldsby sailed into New York harbor at the end of January, 1691, with two companies of regulars and news that Henry Sloughter was coming as royal governor and that several men Leisler had imprisoned for opposition were appointed to the council, Leisler made the fatal mistake of refusing to believe him or turn over the fort to to him. Indeed, he was so fatuous at last as to fire on the king's troops when Ingoldsby marched toward the gate. What might have been a bloody rebellion sputtered for a few days, and then Governor Sloughter's ship arrived. The new executive quickly exerted his authority and threw Leisler and Milborne into the very cells from which their political enemies were released. A special court found both men guilty of treason, and they were hanged.

Word was brought to Sloughter of the intense dissatisfaction of the Iroquois. They had sent a big war party to the north side of the St. Lawrence and spread destruction near the mouth of the Ottawa River until driven off. Now they were impatient over the political dissension which had prevented prosecution of the war by New York. They anticipated new raids from Canada and they wanted both action and supplies from their ally.

The complaints sounded serious enough that Sloughter called the chiefs to council and went up to Albany to meet them on May 27, 1691. Wisely he brought presents from himself and the new monarchs to reassure the chiefs of the strong protective arm of their English father. To second the gesture, Mayor Peter Schuyler stood ready to lead them on a new raid to the St. Lawrence. Their spirits rekindled, one hundred and fifty braves made ready to join one hundred and twenty white volunteers.

Schuyler set off on June 22, collected his Indians, made canoes, and paddled the length of Lake Champlain. Ten miles from Fort Chambly the party left its canoes under guard of twenty-seven men and set out through the woods to pay another visit to La Prairie. The fortified settlement had received early warning of the enemy's intention, and Lieutenant Gov-

ernor Louis Hector de Callières of Montreal promptly crossed
the St. Lawrence with more than four hundred men, red and
white. They camped around the fort for a week, waiting. During a rainstorm on the night of August 1, the Canadians, although well warmed with brandy, sought shelter. Just before
dawn Schuyler attacked. The surprise cost many Canadian
lives as the English chased them into the fort. The garrison
sprang to arms and rushed out only to meet a volley that felled
many more. But as the larger Canadian force rallied, Schuyler
called a retreat. He repulsed a counterattack and then broke
off the engagement, having accomplished his main purpose with
small loss.

To their own surprise the Yorkers and Iroquois were not pursued in the growing light. The commandant at Fort Chambly,
however, had learned of the raid and now laid an ambush along
the forest path of Schuyler's retreat. The Americans blundered
straight into it but, believing the enemy to be a small party,
charged immediately. The unexpected firepower revealed a
body equal in size and sent Schuyler's troops reeling back.
In peril front and rear, they desperately attacked again and in
face-to-face fighting smashed the Canadian line.

"We broke thro' the middle of their body," Schuyler reported, "until we got into their rear trampling upon their dead,
then faced about upon them and fought them a pretty while
close, until we made them give way."

The fire was too hot for some of the Indians on both sides.
Schuyler lost about forty men on the spot, but the Yorkers
carried off their wounded to the canoes and even waited un-
molested for several hours for stragglers before embarking.
They were lucky to get off so easily, for if the forces from La
Prairie and Chambly had pursued, the invaders might have

been annihilated. Governor Frontenac was disappointed when he heard of the action. Schuyler reported his losses at twenty-one whites and twenty-two Indians, plus many wounded. Canadian losses were larger, but no accurate figure is obtainable (Schuyler thought he killed about two hundred French and Indians).

On his return Schuyler was greeted by the news that on July 23 Governor Sloughter had died unexpectedly. Major Ingoldsby was acting as lieutenant governor until the king's pleasure should be known, but the vacancy diminished the war effort. In fact, with the Iroquois somewhat mollified and the French presumably deterred from an offensive move, many New Yorkers felt they could relax. A garrison of one hundred and fifty was maintained at Albany, and if any Iroquois itched to go on the warpath they were welcome to carry out their own raids. They proceeded to do so in the spring, blockading furs from reaching Montreal and keeping Canadian farmers terrorized. And because so few Indians were hunting furs, Albany merchants also suffered.

Intercolonial co-operation was forgotten. Massachusetts, somewhat disillusioned, was heavily in debt for its fiasco. In this temper the colony commissioned an experienced veteran who had crushed King Philip's uprising fifteen years earlier to take the offensive in Maine. Fat but energetic, blustering but with good military judgment, Major Benjamin Church raised three hundred men from Plymouth and Massachusetts Bay and sailed up to Casco Bay early in September, 1691. Marching to the Androscoggin River, he surprised a vacated fort at modern Brunswick. It was inhabited only by squaws and children. Church recovered two English captives and then killed most of the Indians.

The Colonial Wars

Turning up the river forty miles to another Indian fort at modern Lewiston, the expedition killed twenty Indians, rescued seven prisoners, and burned the place. The greatest coup was to capture Chief Moxus, the Norridgewock Abenaki notoriously hostile to the English, but he soon escaped. On the return southward, Church had a minor skirmish, and back at Casco Bay he killed eight or ten Indians at the cost of five men. Re-embarking he stopped at Wells to leave a hundred men under Captain James Converse as a guard. Then Church returned to Boston. Although he had delivered several thrusts and never met defeat, Massachusetts was disappointed in that nothing decisive seemed to have been accomplished.

The march into Maine had its effect, nevertheless. In November the Abenakis sent in a flag of truce to Captain Converse at Wells and asked for a council at the mouth of the Kennebec on November 23. A meeting took place, and ten white captives were turned in. The Abenakis promised to bring their remaining prisoners to Wells next May 1. They also agreed to bury their hatchets against the English. On this note a treaty was signed on November 29, even by the notorious Chief Moxus. The whole coastal area down to Boston breathed easier. A winter free of fear seemed assured.

The truce lasted only until February 5, 1692, when two to three hundred Indians and a few Canadians struck the hamlet of York, south of Wells. Before the startled inhabitants could flee to the fortified houses, forty-eight were killed and seventy-three taken prisoner. The marauders burned the town, except for the four fortified houses, killed the cattle, and carried their captives up to the Kennebec, where several were recovered in the spring. The distraught survivors considered abandoning the town, but Massachusetts sent them help; and in the spring

42

Abenkas didn't bring copt.

three companies of militia under Major Elisha Hutchinson (grandson of the banished Mrs. Anne Hutchinson) patrolled the region.

This protective screen did not prevent an attack on Wells, twelve miles away. May 1 passed without the promised appearance of the Abenakis with their captives. The whole month went by, and a reminder was sent to them. As if in response, on June 10 a mob of four hundred Abenakis under Moxus and a score of Canadians under Captain Portneuf and the Baron de St. Castin descended on the town. Captain Converse had only twenty-nine militiamen, five fortified houses, and two sloops in the creek. The attackers concentrated on the palisaded house occupied by the militia and on the ships. It was a noisy assault but not a determined one. Many insults were exchanged, and the Indians were especially eager to get Converse to emerge from his stronghold. In the afternoon they roamed the area burning houses and the church and slaughtering cattle. Once they tried to burn the sloops with a fire raft but it snagged, while a meager direct attack was driven off. The one inhabitant they had seized at the outset they tortured to death, a warning that only made the defenders more determined. Then, at nightfall, the raiders all withdrew. The Abenaki war spirit had been easily assuaged, even though it was abundantly clear that last fall's treaty was a dead letter.

Sir William Phips returned to Boston with a new charter for the colony. Although it united Plymouth and Maine with Massachusetts Bay, it did not prescribe the hoped for republic, but made the colony royal—with Sir William the newly appointed governor. He concerned himself at once with the suffering settlements in Maine and ordered a stone fort to be built at Pemaquid, his birthplace. Naming Major Church as commander of the militia for Maine, Phips sailed with him and four hundred and fifty men to Pemaquid in August, 1692. While Church ranged against the Indians, Phips laid out a respectable fort to accommodate more than a dozen cannon. When its walls went up, it was named Fort William Henry and a garrison of sixty men was stationed there.

The Abenakis considered this advanced post a direct threat and complained to Governor Frontenac. He promised an expedition to seize it before the end of the year. Such a party did embark by ship under the leadership of Pierre Le Moyne d'Iberville, trained in the French navy and younger brother of Ste. Hélène. When he beheld the stone structure and an armed ship in front of it, he turned around and sailed home. The Abenakis were disgusted, as was even old Frontenac.

The governor may have been heartened, as many habitants were, by an incident up the St. Lawrence. A French officer who had been granted a seigniory called Verchères, about twenty miles below Montreal on the south shore, supervised a settlement protected by a stockade and blockhouse. While he and his wife were absent, an Iroquois war party attacked the place on October 22. Madeleine Jarret de Verchères, fourteen-year-old daughter of the seignior, was working in the fields with most of the tenants when the Indians came in view. She fled under fire to the stockade with a workman and barred the gate against their pursuers. Inside, Madeleine found only her two younger brothers, an old man, two soldiers hiding in the blockhouse, and some women and small children. With spirit she goaded the soldiers into taking to the ramparts, armed her brothers and the two men, and soon had seven muskets returning fire and holding the raiders at bay. That night a neighboring family sneaked into the fort. Madeleine inspired the disconsolate and weary by her example of resolute courage. The half-dozen men and boys called to each other at night along the firing platform to convince the Iroquois that a strong garrison held out. For a week, until relief arrived, the defenders clung to their post.

Massachusetts was now distracted by its witchcraft delusion. Inspired by their religious leaders, the less educated readily succumbed to the preposterous hysteria. Innocent if at times eccentric persons were accused of fantastic crimes and influence, and twenty were executed—for their own good, of course. After the terror had run its course and rational minds prevailed again, the presiding judge in several of the cases recanted his action, but the local clergy were unwilling to concede that the devil had not been active in their midst. So credulous a people would readily believe any partial truth about the French.

In New York a new governor, Benjamin Fletcher, arrived near the end of August, 1692, with money for Indian presents if not for provincial defense. He was vigorous in war measures, but, like many other officeholders of the time, he used his position to line his pockets—by granting vast tracts of land to favorites and by allowing pirates to use the harbor. Hastening to Albany, Fletcher met the Iroquois chiefs, thanked them for their raids this year, and distributed gifts. Ingoldsby was put in command there. Already heavily taxed, the New Yorkers felt they could do no more to mount another offensive. Queen Mary wrote to several royal governors urging them to help New York carry on the war, but only Virginia and Maryland responded, and they sent money, not men. The requisition system proved unsatisfactory.

Time was overdue for a counterstroke from Canada. It came

in February, 1693. Frontenac equipped a force of about four hundred regulars and militia and two hundred mission Indians to move against the Mohawk towns. The expedition, under Mantet and Courtemanche, appeared suddenly on February 8 and burned three villages. Although the warriors were out hunting, the French took about three hundred prisoners and destroyed the tribe's food supplies. All this pillaging required several days, and Albany got word promptly. Major Ingoldsby procrastinated, seeking more militia before he would march. Finally Peter Schuyler set off on February 13 with two hundred and seventy-five whites and about as many Indians and caught up with the invaders four days later. He started a running fight that cost the French between thirty and eighty killed and many wounded. Moreover, while defending themselves on the move, they lost most of their Mohawk captives.

Meanwhile, Governor Fletcher had rushed men from New York City as far as Schenectady, when he heard Schuyler was returning. The Mohawks were as much gratified by his exertions as they were thankful for Schuyler's prompt action that saved their families. The governor ordered corn for the Mohawks to replace their loss, and the warriors decided to build new towns.

Having demonstrated that he could strike the Iroquois at will, Frontenac now put out a peace feeler in hope of neutralizing them. There was a peace faction among the tribes ready to listen. Several chiefs conferred with Frontenac in Quebec and sought a peace that would include the English as well, but Frontenac refused. He demanded the return of all prisoners as a prerequisite to any treaty. At another conference with Governor Fletcher in July, the chiefs made it clear that while respecting him they must listen to the French in order to keep them out of their country, since the English could give so little help. If, on the other hand, the English would undertake an offensive, they would cease their peace talk. The Oneidas in particular were wavering. The governor understood their jibe at him, but with fine oratory and broad promises he persuaded them to have no dealings with the French. Frontenac continued to tamper with them and kept Albany anxious.

As autumn approached, Virginia and Maryland sent £900 to New York, and New Jersey contributed men and money. New England rightfully felt it had its own frontier to guard, and Quaker Pennsylvania would do nothing. When Fletcher arranged another intercolonial conference for defense, those who attended used the absence of others as an excuse for reaching no agreement.

The Maine frontier enjoyed a respite throughout 1693, chiefly because Captain Converse ranged the country with three hundred and fifty added levies. He also built another stone fort on the west side of Saco Bay. The Indians feared him and moved inland. In August thirteen chiefs came to Fort William Henry at Pemaquid to talk peace. They agreed to release all captives, to trade with the English again, and to obey the English Crown. To be sure, they had promised part of this the year before and failed to keep their word, but Massachusetts could only hope that this time they might mean it.

They did, for a year. Then, aroused by the Sieur de Villieu, new commandant at Penobscot, a band of two hundred and fifty Abenakis moved down to Oyster Bay (Durham), New Hampshire, in July, 1694. Of twelve fortified houses, the Indians destroyed five and killed or carried off more than ninety inhabitants. The force then ravaged the coast up as far as York, killing lone individuals. As a result, when three Indians came

Into Christ Ideology // French Ideology

into the Saco fort and four into Fort William Henry feigning innocence of the raid, they were seized as hostages and sent to Boston. One of them, Chief Bomaseen, explained to an inquisitive Puritan divine that he was indeed a Christian, that he understood the Virgin Mary was a French lady whose son Jesus was murdered by Englishmen, that he had risen to heaven, and all who wanted to earn his favor must avenge his death. This theological digest confirmed Boston's dark suspicions of the evil-minded Jesuit missionaries.

In Europe Louis XIV now realized that 1693 had been his high-water mark. He had won as many neighboring cities as he could expect, and having been stopped he was ready to make peace to hold on to his gains. William III was not so agreeable, having demands of his own, and so the war rumbled on.

In the spring of 1695 one of the Indian hostages in Boston was released to arrange an exchange of prisoners. A meeting was scheduled near Pemaquid on May 20, and eight white captives were produced. A second parley was set for mid-June, but the Massachusetts commissioners did not bring their other hostages, the Indians refused to treat with them, and the council collapsed. Fighting broke out again, and in the next three months about forty settlers were killed or captured.

The strained atmosphere of not war, not peace, hovered over the New York frontier throughout 1694 and 1695. Neither side had the resources to prepare an offensive. Canada was just getting food supplies and bare replacements for its regular troops, and the English also had not obtained much help from home. The Iroquois remained on the fence, now talking with Fletcher, now sending messages to Frontenac. It was Frontenac who broke off the inconclusive talk in January, 1695, by an-

Sir William Phips. Artist unknown

Colonel Benjamin Church. From a nineteenth-century engraving

nouncing that he was going to repair and garrison Fort Frontenac, at the east end of Lake Ontario. The Iroquois were alarmed but nothing happened. A faction in Canada under Intendant Chapigny opposed Frontenac's move for fear the fort would become a center of illegal trade by the governor's friends. Frontenac felt obliged to protect his Indian allies and repel English encroachment, and he also believed that the only way to accomplish these ends was by occupying the interior through forts and trading posts. England finally sent two more companies of regulars for duty at Albany, but Fletcher could not answer the plea of the Onondagas for five hundred men and artillery.

THE LAST BLOWS

The unnatural lull came to an end in the summer of 1696, with a double offensive rolling out of Canada. From Quebec, Iberville sailed in two ships with two companies of soldiers around to New Brunswick's St. John River, where he picked up fifty Indians. Then at Penobscot the vessels took on Villieu and St. Castin and led a brigade of canoes containing two hundred Indians. The flotilla proceeded down to Pemaquid once more and on July 14, 1696, summoned the commandant, Captain Pascoe Chubb, to surrender Fort William Henry. He had ninety-five men in garrison and fifteen good cannon, but the next day—after the French had landed cannon and mortars and lobbed a few shells over the walls—he gave up. When the gates were opened, the Indians killed a few soldiers before Iberville intervened and moved the Massachusetts troops to an island. Then the victors plundered the fort and systematically demolished it. Three days later they withdrew to Penobscot. Captain Chubb was arrested and cashiered by Massachusetts; a year and a half later he and his wife were killed by Indians at their home.

To retaliate, Massachusetts raised five hundred men and again called on Major Church. Three British ships which had been sent over to help, joined by two local vessels, carried the militia to Penobscot. Both French and Indians were gone, but the invaders found and captured one small boat with Villieu and twenty-three Frenchmen aboard. Church later marched up the coast to the Bay of Fundy, killing a few Indians on the way and laying waste the settlements he found, but he did not encounter any organized resistance.

Iberville had transferred his operations to Newfoundland, where he killed or captured the American fishermen settled on its eastern coast. Still full of fight, he embarked early the following year for Hudson Bay, bested three British warships, and seized the post of Fort Nelson.

After Iberville had left Quebec, seventy-six-year-old Governor Frontenac assembled at Montreal two thousand regulars, militia, and Indians and paddled up the river to Fort Frontenac. From there, carried in a chair by his Indians, he invaded central New York on July 26, 1696, moving into the heart of the Onondaga country. The Onondagas fled before such superior forces, leaving their village in flames. The Canadians destroyed their standing corn and food supplies. The neighboring Oneidas sued for peace, but Frontenac answered that they must then move to Canada. To enforce his demand he sent seven hundred men under Philippe de Rigaud, Marquis de Vaudreuil, to burn their town.

As soon as Governor Fletcher learned of the invasion, he wanted to rush troops westward, but he had no funds to provision them. By the time he was able to borrow money, the

French had gone. All he could do was provide corn for the two tribes. His plight made clear to the Iroquois that New York would not back its promises to protect them. The governor's council accused Fletcher of not filling vacancies in the four companies of regulars so that he could appropriate their pay to himself. At a powwow in September the chiefs again demanded expulsion of the French from Canada as their only safeguard and insisted on sending a message of their own directly to King William. Fletcher was sufficiently worried about his red allies as well as the French to decide to spend the winter in Albany.

These two hit-and-run attacks of 1696 were destined to be the last major strokes of the war. A French squadron of fifteen ships reached Newfoundland the next summer for the purpose of supporting an invasion army in a plan to burn Boston, but since provisions had run low, the admiral would proceed no farther. The Iroquois again offered to make peace with Frontenac, but not with his Indian allies. Though Louis XIV favored such a settlement, the governor spurned it.

Maine's Indians carried on some raids in 1697 from Saco to Kittery. One story is still recounted. A war party of Abenakis fell on several farmhouses near Haverhill, Massachusetts, on March 15. In one lived the Dustin family. Mrs. Hannah Dustin had just been delivered of her eighth child the week before and was being nursed by one Mary Neff. Mr. Dustin had taken the seven children to the field with him. When the savages struck, he sent the children running to a fortified house while he started to rescue his wife. The savages turned on him, and he found he could only retreat and keep firing to give his children the time they needed. Mrs. Dustin, her baby, and the nurse were carried off and the house set afire.

Because the baby cried, a warrior seized it by the feet and

bashed its head against a tree. The benumbed mother and frightened nurse were driven deeper into the forest where they soon came to a rendezvous of more Indians and captive neighbors. Some of the prisoners were now killed—there were twenty-seven victims altogether of the raid—and others were divided among the captors. Mrs. Dustin, Mary Neff, and a neighbor lad were assigned to a party of two warriors, three squaws, and seven children. They continued northward, hunting along the way. Night and morning the Catholic Indians prayed with their rosaries. The captives carried heavy loads and were frequently abused. The women were told that when they reached the home village they would be stripped and made to run the gauntlet. After six weeks en route Mrs. Dustin decided that a break for freedom must be made. She whispered her plan to the nurse and the boy. On the night of April 29, after all the Indians were sleeping around a dying fire, the three prisoners got up noiselessly and each procured a hatchet. In concert they moved around the circle of twelve Indians and killed all but one old squaw and a boy, who ran off screaming into the woods. Then they waited by their victims until dawn, when the frugal Hannah Dustin proceeded to scalp each one. With their grisly trophies they started back home and made it safely to Haverhill. Massachusetts promptly paid them £50 bounty for the ten scalps, and Mr. Dustin was reunited with his truly formidable wife.

The war came to an end in Europe on September 30, 1697, with the signing of the Treaty of Ryswick. France recognized William as the legitimate ruler of England, made commercial concessions to the Dutch, returned Lorraine to its duke but kept the city of Strasbourg. In America all conquests were restored. The boundary between Acadia and Maine was left to future determination, as were the borders of Hudson Bay and the allegiance of the Iroquois. In brief, everything reverted to the status before France had threatened it. The "balance of power," an old idea in Europe, was henceforth to include a balance of strength in colonies and overseas trade. News of the peace reached New York and Boston in December, but not Montreal and Quebec until the next February.

Casualties of the war are impossible to count. The available evidence suggests that at least six hundred and fifty Anglo-Americans were killed or died in captivity, mostly in New England. Albany County in New York suffered eighty-four dead and sixteen captured, but four hundred moved away during the war, a decrease in population of 25 per cent. The French got off much lighter; apparently about three hundred were killed. The Indians suffered too: those allied with the French probably lost something more than one hundred, but the Iroquois may have mourned as many as thirteen hundred dead from battle and disease, although half that sum is a more realistic figure.

Governor Fletcher having been recalled, and Governor Phips having died, Great Britain decided once more to combine the governments of Massachusetts, New York, and New Hampshire to unify their defense efforts. The Earl of Bellomont, an Irish supporter of William and honest if impatient, was named to the governorship. He arrived at New York in April, 1698, and immediately sent Peter Schuyler to Quebec with a copy of the treaty and orders to arrange an exchange of prisoners. Schuyler took with him the French prisoners and promised to procure Indian and French captives from the Iroquois. In return he asked for the English and Iroquois prisoners detained in Canada.

The Colonial Wars

Frontenac balked. Wanting to alienate the Iroquois from English domination, he declared that they were rebellious subjects of Louis and he would deal directly with them. When he threatened another invasion of New York to carry out his intention, Governor Bellomont sent him a sharp letter of rebuke and challenge. Stubborn and fuming, Frontenac fell ill and died in November. Superior to his royal master in many qualities, including judgment, he was the strongest governor ever to rule Canada.

He was succeeded by his lieutenant, Governor Callières of Montreal, who released all the Iroquois prisoners and sent three Canadians to receive French captives from the Iroquois. To their surprise, only thirteen women and children were willing to go home; the men liked the free, primitive life and the dusky maidens. The Iroquois were then invited to a mammoth peace congress with the western and Christian tribes at Montreal in 1701. Several hundred of the non-Iroquois Indians, from thirty tribes, appeared and dutifully brought their Iroquois prisoners. The Iroquois delegates had conveniently "forgotten" to bring their Algonquin prisoners, but insisted on receiving their own and promised to send up their captives later—which they never did. Callières was satisfied to ask only that the Iroquois agree to stay neutral in any future war.

Who won the war? Since England and her allies had declared war on France, and Louis initiated proposals for peace, it might be hastily assumed that France had lost. Yet she gave up no old territory in Europe or in America. It is more accurate to say that Louis' ambitions were checked for the first time. He had failed to improve France's power or to expand her eastern border as much as he wished. Having been halted, he was glad to cease an expensive war—and wait for a more favorable opportunity to renew it.

England, on the other hand, enjoyed only the dubious satisfaction of having thwarted the wilful Louis XIV. What she had gained is difficult to see. If her prestige in Europe was elevated, the war had not brought her colonies closer to her. Indeed, they felt that they had been left not only to defend their northern borders but to create and support every offensive campaign. Only four Independent Companies had been sent over to fight. Yet the theory undergirding royal colonies was that in return for allegiance the king extended protection—which had not been demonstrated. The fabric of empire now had a torn seam. The Lords of Trade, on whom responsibility for colonial affairs had been thrust, were convinced that the colonies had men and means to drive the French out of Canada, if only they would forget their jealousies of one another and of royal prerogative.

Who won? Perhaps it was the Iroquois, despite the cost in lives. Early in the war they had renounced independence for security, and when it was not provided, they were able to recover their independence from the English and make a separate peace with the French. This position left them to be courted once more by each power. They clung to the English for protection and gifts while pleasing the French by staying neutral. Their power might decline as both European nations moved inland, but their adroit policy preserved them on their lands until the end of the American Revolution.

Knowing the future we can see certain notions emerging during this struggle in North America. Perhaps the most important was the implanting of the idea in Albany and Boston and the Iroquois villages that the only way to achieve permanent peace was to push the French off the continent. In two generations this tantalizing hope would mature to a widespread and passionate conviction. The other idea was even more amorphous. Intercolonial co-operation had been attempted by some of the English provinces, and although the joint military effort had failed, at least there had been official discussions. The participants were dimly aware that they had certain common problems, such as defense, and that the burden of the solutions might be lightened by some sort of joint action.

What is more interesting, the two ideas were related, and were already beginning to strengthen each other.

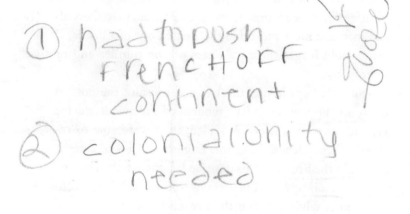

① had to push
    frenchoff
    continent
② colonial unity
    needed

ch 2 summary

III

Attempts at Military Co-operation
Queen Anne's War

Checked by war, Louis XIV remained eager to extend his empire for the sake of prestige. Yet he pursued almost every countervailing course: he would not let the Huguenots, who would have migrated by the thousands, enter Canada; he favored the policy of restricting interior posts and discouraging settlement in order to leave the fur hunting and the proselyting by Catholic missionaries undisturbed; and of course he would not suffer self-government or take pains to insure competent autocratic rule. He had no vision. The ambitious or farseeing empire builders had to persuade him to let them make their moves. Two of these men, lieutenants of Governor Frontenac, succeeded at this time: Iberville and Cadillac.

Returning to France at the end of the war, Iberville immediately set about winning royal permission to establish a colony at the mouth of the Mississippi, where La Salle had failed. He sailed in October, 1698, with a group of settlers and his much younger brother, Jean Baptiste Le Moyne de Bienville, eighteen years old. In the Gulf of Mexico they passed Pensacola Bay where the Spaniards were erecting Fort San Carlos to mark Florida's westward expansion. Iberville found the mouth of the Mississippi but preferred a site on Biloxi Bay, farther east and one hundred miles west of Pensacola. The Spaniards protested this proximity, but the issue was quashed at home. Young Bienville explored the whole region, cultivating the friendship of the Indians, and the brothers decided in 1702 to transfer the colony to Mobile Bay, hardly fifty miles from Pensacola. They began by erecting Fort Louis.

Antoine de la Mothe Cadillac, a voluble Gascon more clever than wise, more covetous than inspiring, had lived at Port Royal and in Maine. By his friend and patron, Governor Frontenac, he had been given the command of Fort de Buade (St. Ignace) at Michilimackinac in 1694. The two men shared a dislike of the Jesuits and a faith in interior development as the means of extending the empire. When the king ordered the western posts abandoned at the end of the war, Captain Cadillac descended to Quebec, and on Frontenac's death returned to France. Imaginative and confident, he persuaded the king's ministers that a post was needed, nevertheless, on the Detroit River to protect the fur trade from the English and the Iroquois. Accordingly he was granted permission to found a settlement, to govern it, and later to enjoy a monopoly of its fur trade.

Back in Canada he gathered a hundred men and set out in 1701. On the northwest shore of the river connecting Lake Ste. Claire with Lake Erie, he laid out a simple stockade with a water gate that he named Fort Pontchartrain. He had brought along a Recollet father, and a Jesuit because he had to. There were no Indian villages in the vicinity closer than the Chippewas at Saginaw Bay. So he invited the tribes at Michilimackinac to settle near him and soon had neighboring towns of Ottawas, Hurons, Potawatomis, and Foxes. Needless to add, the Jesuits at Michilimackinac were furious at this triple threat: a man who undermined their colonial policy for France, who favored their rivals, and who stole their potential converts.

The encirclement of the English colonies that New York's Governor Dongan had foreseen was now becoming obvious to everyone in America, though not in Britain. New France was bending in a giant arc from Fort Frontenac to Fort Pontchartrain, through missions among the Illinois Confederation, and down the Mississippi to a firm anchor on the Gulf of Mexico. Yet these two new western settlements were to remain secure under the French fleur-de-lis in the coming war.

Human mortality now upset the delicate balance of power in Europe. When Charles II, the last Hapsburg king of Spain, died in 1700 without issue, two claimants appeared for the throne. Austria supported another Hapsburg, nephew of the dead king and son of Austria's Leopold I. France, or rather Louis XIV, wanted to place his grandson Philip, grandnephew of Charles, on the throne. At the last moment Charles had changed his will in favor of Philip, provided that the crowns of France and Spain never were set on one head. But after Charles's death and Philip's accession, Louis recognized the youngster's right of succession to the French throne. In alarm England and Holland supported Austria in her refusal to accept Philip as legitimate, fearful, in part, that France might gain control of the Spanish colonies. France picked up allies in two German states and one Italian duchy. Spain—the plum—was divided in its allegiance but was brought into the coming war by France.

Then the ousted king of England, James II, died in France, and Louis in violation of the Treaty of Ryswick committed his second act of treachery by recognizing James's Catholic son as the rightful king of England. This was too much for William; he activated the Grand Alliance toward a second war with France, even though Parliament had reduced the British army. In March, 1702, William died and was succeeded by Anne, the Protestant daughter of James and sister of William's late consort. Anne joined with Holland and Austria in declaring war on May 4, 1702—the War of the Spanish Succession. They were augmented by Prussia and Portugal.

War in America was resumed before the previous one had grown cold or its peace terms fulfilled. The new conflict, slow in getting under way, was called Queen Anne's War here. Military action was confined to New England, Carolina, Florida, and the West Indies. Ironically, New York escaped entirely from invasions and raids in this war because of the neutrality of the Iroquois—a development that New York had done its best to prevent! By their assertion of independence the Iroquois had made it worth more to Canada to leave New York alone than to antagonize the province and risk retaliation by the Indians. New York certainly was not neutral in spirit, but was politically sophisticated enough to believe that only a military force from England directed against Quebec could defeat the Canadians.

Action in North America flared first in the West Indies. Upon receipt of news of the declaration of war, the British governor of the Leeward Islands had no trouble seizing the French half of St. Christopher Island (St. Kitts) in July, 1702.

The next spring he laid siege to Guadeloupe but was unsuccessful, after losing several hundred men in action and from disease.

Spaniards were next to feel the English sword. In October, 1702, Governor James Moore of Carolina, a planter and adventurer, gathered some five hundred militia and three hundred Indians, mostly Yamasees, and sailed southward from Port Royal. Their goal was to take Fort San Marcos at St. Augustine "before it be strengthened with French forces," and the men were promised plunder. The squadron turned in at St. Johns River, and the force captured several outposts on the approach to St. Augustine. It ransacked the deserted town, burning many houses, but the moated stone fort containing the garrison and fourteen hundred inhabitants was more than the Carolinians bargained for. Moore sent to Jamaica for cannon, but they failed to arrive. Governor Zuñiga withstood a siege of seven weeks, and when two Spanish warships appeared on Christmas day, Moore decided to retreat to his relief ships at St. Johns River. The expedition cost £8,500, for which Carolina issued paper currency.

A year later, having lost the governorship, Colonel Moore proposed a second expedition, against the Apalachee settlements west of St. Augustine. The Assembly gave reluctant approval but specified that the force must pay its own way. Moore could enlist only fifty militia, but he raised about a thousand Indians and after a long march won a pitched battle. Though he did not attack Fort San Luis (Tallahassee), he broke up thirteen dependent missions—never restored—and carried off nearly a thousand mission Indians as slaves. Another thirteen hundred were resettled along the Savannah River as a buffer. Moore lost only four whites and fifteen Indians, and the expedition more than paid for itself in loot and slaves.

The Colonial Wars

Florida's jealousy of the nearby French changed to alliance against a common enemy, the English. France in turn saw Florida as Louisiana's bastion. There would be a reckoning with Carolina.

Farther north political changes were rife. Governor Bellomont had died, and Queen Anne sent over a cousin, Lord Cornbury, as governor of New York. He was a drunk and a grafter who declined into a detested failure. Massachusetts and New Hampshire were combined under Joseph Dudley, Harvard 1665 but an apostate son of Massachusetts Anglicized by his long residence in England. He loved power and was a sophisticated man of the world. He had also served as chief justice in the trial of Jacob Leisler. The Canadian governor, Callières, also died in May, 1703, and was succeeded by the Marquis de Vaudreuil, a veteran of the last war who had taken Callières' place as governor of Montreal. He was a French aristocrat, a capable leader who held his office until his death in 1725.

Governor Dudley called the Abenaki chiefs to council in June, 1703, and they swore to keep the peace. But within a month Governor Vaudreuil had assembled some five hundred of the tribe and sent them against Maine under the Sieur de Beaubassin. They divided into half a dozen war parties to strike simultaneously on August 10 from Wells to Saco to Casco Bay. At Wells thirty-nine inhabitants were killed or captured. At Saco and other places, a hundred were taken or killed. Chief Moxus led the attack on the fort at Casco, which was under the command of Major John March. Three soldiers, drawn from the fort by trickery, were killed, but the fort held out until relieved, even after Beaubassin brought up his other parties.

Memories of the preceding war flooded back; was it all to be relived? Two months later another raid in the area cost eighteen killed or captured at Black Point, and six killed at York. The French were successful in so committing the Abenakis that the English were unlikely to make peace with them.

There was some relief as winter came on, but the heaviest blow of all was in preparation—the sack of Deerfield, on the Connecticut River in Massachusetts. The little town already had a history of vicissitudes: it was almost wiped out in 1676 during King Philip's War, and in 1694 a raiding party of French and Indians had been beaten off. As a result several of its forty-one houses were fortified, and a sentry had been posted nightly since war resumed. On the last night of February, 1704, a mixed party of two hundred Canadians and a hundred and forty Abenakis and Christianized Indians of Caughnawaga attacked. They were under the command of Captain Hertel de Rouville, veteran of the last war.

The village contained two hundred and seventy souls and twenty soldiers from neighboring towns, all asleep. The surprise was complete, but the slaughter not as heavy in the chaotic nightmare as might be expected. Thirty-eight inhabitants were killed, and seventeen houses went up in flames, but half the others found refuge in fortified places. There was enough resistance for the Indians to lose eight warriors, and the Canadians three. One hundred and eleven prisoners were taken and sent north at daylight. The surviving villagers pursued the retreating raiders and inflicted thirty casualties but lost nine more of their own people without recovering any of the captives.

On the three-hundred-mile journey to Montreal, sixteen of the prisoners were killed and two starved to death. The most famous captives were the family of the Reverend John Williams. The baby was killed at the outset, and Mrs. Williams was killed on the march, along with their Negro slave. Three sons, two daughters, and Mr. Williams survived the long trek. Jesuit priests tried to convert the children and even hounded the intractable minister. Eventually almost all the Deerfield survivors were ransomed and exchanged with Massachusetts, except for a few children, including Eunice Williams, whom even Governor Vaudreuil could not obtain from the Indians. She remained with the Caughnawaga converts, turned Catholic, married one of the Indians, and had two children. Thirty-six years later she was reunited with her brothers and sister for a visit, but the gulf was so great that she returned to Caughnawaga to live out the remainder of her eighty-nine years. Largely through the publicity attending the abduction of the Williams family the Deerfield raid has been kept alive for more than two hundred and fifty years as the most widely known event of Queen Anne's War. The good minister published an account of his ordeal in 1707 that has gone through sixteen editions.

Massachusetts raised five hundred and fifty men under the redoubtable Colonel Benjamin Church, now sixty-five, not to pursue the Deerfield victims but to strike at the Abenakis from Penobscot to Port Royal. They sailed out of Boston on May 21, 1704. Raiding along the way, they killed a few Indians here and there and captured others, including the half-breed daughter of Baron de St. Castin, who had returned to France. The expedition burned Grand Pré on the Bay of Fundy and reached Port Royal, but at a council of war on July 14 decided it was too strong to be taken. The force returned home with a hundred prisoners, having lost only six men and achieved little. This was the fifth and last Indian expedition of Colonel Church.

Massachusetts was understandably irritated by New York's inaction and immunity. What was worse, Albany merchants were carrying on a quiet trade with St. Lawrence River Indians, and plunder taken on raids in Maine, New Hampshire, and Massachusetts turned up in Albany shops.

A lull now developed, and it was Governor Vaudreuil who opened negotiations for an exchange of prisoners in May, 1705. He had one hundred and seventeen and he knew of seventy more among the Indians. Massachusetts sent up to Quebec seventy prisoners but got only sixty in return. Vaudreuil pretended that his Indians were independent allies whom he could not force to give up their captives. In ill humor Massachusetts now accused its own commissioner, Samuel Vetch, of prolonging the exchange business in order to carry on trade with the enemy. Actually Vetch was carrying a secret letter to Vaudreuil from Governor Dudley proposing a truce of neutrality between the two provinces. Vaudreuil received it favorably but insisted on two conditions: that New York and the other northern English colonies be included, and that the English give up their fishing off Newfoundland. The first might be difficult to comply with; the second was impossible. Besides, Vaudreuil on his part would not agree to collect and surrender the prisoners in the hands of his Indians.

THE MIRAGE OF HELP FROM HOME

In the summer of 1706 the war came to life again in the South. Iberville had left Mobile for the West Indies and already captured the islands of Nevis and St. Kitts in April. Before he could extend his conquests he died of fever. Spain and France were devising measures to revenge themselves for the attacks on St. Augustine and Apalachee. Five French privateers were engaged to carry Spanish troops from Havana and St. Augustine to attack Charleston, South Carolina.

Anticipating such a raid, Charlestonians had called in militia and built stronger fortifications. Even so, the town might have been sacked by a more determined and better-commanded enemy. The Spaniards were poorly led, their landing parties were repulsed, and two hundred and thirty of them were taken. Then Colonel William Rhett, with an improvised squadron, drove off the French ships.

Aroused and encouraged, the Carolinians decided on an offensive against the centers of Spanish and French power. A few of them raised several hundred Talapoosas (of Alabama) to attack Pensacola in the summer of 1707. The attackers killed eleven Spaniards and captured fifteen, but failed to take Fort San Carlos. In November Pensacola was hit again and siege begun. It did not prosper, and the invaders were ready to give up when Bienville brought relief from Mobile to the garrison and hastened their decision. South Carolina also had its martial eye on Mobile, but was unable to rouse the neighboring Indians or unify its own leaders of the enterprise. On both sides the southern offensive expired.

Governor Dudley had sought help from England to capture Port Royal in Acadia and obtained nothing. England clung stubbornly to the faith that the colonists could and should prosecute their own war. Colonel Church's failure kept the issue hot. Although some Boston merchants were trading illegally with the inhabitants, Boston fishermen were frequently driven away by Port Royal privateers. Finally in 1707 Dudley asked the General Court to authorize and underwrite an enterprise against Port Royal. Two regiments were called for, vessels were to be impressed, an English frigate in port was to be used, and neighboring colonies were to be invited to join.

The expedition sailed on May 13. New Hampshire contributed 60 men, and Rhode Island 80. With the two Massachusetts regiments there was a grand total of 1,076 soldiers and about 450 sailors. Colonel John March was the commander, facing a military problem quite different from his frontier service. The troops were landed in two parties and without much trouble drove the advanced French forces back into the fort, commanded by Governor Daniel d'Auger de Subercase.

The New Englanders ranged themselves in a long semicircle and camped. Then they disintegrated into a wrangling, unmanageable mob. It developed that the officers did not know how to conduct a siege, and the soldiers, losing all confidence in them, reverted to the civilians they actually were. After three councils of war about proceeding or giving up, the noble force decamped for Casco Bay. Colonel March sent an apologetic message to Governor Dudley, who, though deeply disappointed, demanded another attempt at once. Accordingly Dudley dispatched to Maine a hundred recruits, another frigate, and three members of the provincial council to advise March.

The expedition returned to Port Royal in August and found that the French also had been reinforced. For a week there was repeated skirmishing in the open, with several casualties, but no decision. Once more the New Englanders withdrew. Boston was loud in its condemnation and demanded court-martial proceedings, but with officers accusing one another there were hardly enough left to serve as judges. The discreditable wrangling eventually dissipated itself.

Border raids resumed in 1708. In midsummer Governor Vaudreuil put together a force of one hundred Canadians and three hundred Christian Indians under Hertel de Rouville, of Deerfield fame. They were to be joined en route by eastern Indians and sweep the frontier once more. But the reinforcements did not appear, and many of the mission Indians turned back after experiencing what they considered to be evil omens. With his force reduced almost by half, De Rouville decided to strike at Haverhill, Massachusetts, on the north side of the Merrimac River. The village contained about thirty houses, perhaps one hundred and fifty people, and thirty militia in a picket fort.

Just before dawn on August 29 the French and Indians struck. They met a spirited resistance (it was Hannah Dustin's town), and most of the inhabitants fired from their houses. The raiders tried to burn them out but were not successful. Stubborn fighting persisted for several hours. Relief troops came and tried to ambush the enemy, but killed only nine and wounded eighteen. After the attackers withdrew, the village counted up sixteen dead and three taken prisoner.

Late in 1706 Samuel Vetch had embarked for England. A thirty-eight-year-old Scot, married to Robert Livingston's daughter, he was a newcomer to Massachusetts commerce. But he had seen enough of the war to become convinced that nothing effective against Canada could be accomplished without military aid and leadership from home. The idea was prevalent in New York, of course, but Vetch had the energy and persuasiveness to present "the glorious enterprise" to influential government officials. There was something in it for himself as well. However, it took him two years to extract a favorable decision. He promised that twenty-five hundred colonial troops would co-operate if two battalions of regulars and six warships were dispatched from England with a commander in chief to lead the attack on Quebec.

Governor Dudley supported the idea, and so did Lord Lovelace, who was being sent to New York as governor to replace the corrupt Cornbury. The Board of Trade was slowly convinced by the end of 1708, and its recommendation was adopted by the ministry and the queen in February, 1709. For his pains Vetch was given a colonel's commission to direct colonial preparations and was promised the governorship of Canada after it was taken. With Colonel Francis Nicholson, recently governor of Virginia, Vetch sailed for Boston.

Fifteen hundred men from New York, New Jersey, Connecticut, and Pennsylvania, including the regular Independent Companies, were to rendezvous at Albany in May for an advance on Montreal. The Iroquois were to be brought into the campaign if possible. New England was to raise a thousand men to join with the English forces for an attack by sea on Quebec and Port Royal. Vetch was effective in arousing enthusiasm in all the northern colonies except Quaker Pennsylvania.

Despite the sudden death of Governor Lovelace, New York moved with alacrity under Lieutenant Governor Ingoldsby and abandoned its neutrality. John Schuyler was sent off to the Iroquois with gifts. Colonel Nicholson was accepted to command the forces gathering at Albany. Never had the northern colonies co-operated so harmoniously and energetically, for they were all convinced that driving the French out of North America was the only means of achieving permanent peace. Although Pennsylvania had refused to furnish men, volunteers from the other colonies more than offset the defection. Everything was in readiness and anticipation high, but the British fleet and troops did not appear.

June . . . July . . . August passed, while trade was at a standstill and the numerous troops had to be supported and occupied. Colonel Nicholson cut a wagon road north of Albany, built two forts, and took his troops up to the head of Lake Champlain. Finally, in September, demobilization was ordered.

69

At last, in October, the despondent Vetch received brief word from London that the expedition had been "laid aside." Nothing more. Even this letter had not been sent until August (the decision had been made by the end of May), and on a ship that did not proceed directly to America. Such was the indifference of the ministry to all the colonial planning and expenditure it had authorized. One lesson the colonies now learned was to keep an agent at the English court for prompt transmission of information.

Disillusioned representatives of Massachusetts, New Hampshire, Connecticut, and Rhode Island, along with the principal military officers, met at Vetch's urging in Rehoboth, Rhode Island. The New York Assembly was too disgusted to take part. Swallowing their resentment, the delegates drafted a petition to the queen urging that the expedition be ordered for next year. Meanwhile, they decided to move against Port Royal at once, using British ships then in colonial harbors. But the ship captains refused to participate in any colonial expedition. All that happened was that Colonel Nicholson sailed home with the petition, and New York sent over Colonel Peter Schuyler with four Mohawks to add color to the plea and also bring back to the neutral Iroquois an impression of the queen's might.

In London Nicholson was duly authorized to command colonial forces and five hundred British marines in an attack on Port Royal—not Quebec—transportation and provisions to be furnished by the colonies. Vetch was to remain as administrator of the conquered area. Nicholson returned to Boston in July, 1710, and preparations for the more limited objective were pushed. The expedition sailed in September. With a meager garrison, Governor Subercase had no choice but to surrender, on October 2. Port Royal was rechristened Annapolis Royal, and Vetch assumed the governorship over five hundred local inhabitants and an undefined area. For garrison duty England sent over the Fortieth Regiment. Subercase and the French troops were transported to France. Governor Vaudreuil, however, was not reconciled to the loss of Acadia and urged the inhabitants who wished to leave to stay there and even encouraged the missionary priests to keep the Indians antagonistic toward the English.

The victorious Nicholson returned again to England to urge the old project of the conquest of Canada, this time facing a new ministry of Tories. Once more his argument was supported by Vetch and the other governors, including the new executive of New York, Robert Hunter, an able, honest, and healthy governor for a change. A Canadian conquest appealed to the Tories to offset the prestige gained by the Whigs from the Duke of Marlborough's triumphs on the Continent. They were even willing to bear the cost of dispatching regulars to America.

Preparations, in 1711, were secret but late in starting. The weary governors in America once more met together in June and accepted quotas of troops for two armies: one to gather again at Albany under Nicholson and advance on Montreal, the other under Vetch to accompany the British regulars against Quebec. Admiral Sir Hovenden Walker arrived promptly at Boston before the end of June with more than sixty ships and an army of five thousand under General John Hill. America had seen nothing like it before. Walker disliked his assignment and was pessimistic; Hill had no opinions because he had never held a command before. Neither one's temper was eased by the fractious spirit of suspicion and grumbling exhibited by the assemblies and the people, where enthusiasm and helpfulness were expected. But these people remembered with distaste the failure of 1709, the arrogance of British officials, and a ministry indifferent to colonial efforts.

New York's Governor Hunter perceived an attitude of independence that government must consider and overcome, or there would be future trouble in imperial relations. A French writer predicted that if Canada were conquered, the Anglo-Americans "will then unite, shake off the yoke of the English monarchy, and erect themselves into a democracy." No one took him seriously, of course.

The impressive expedition sailed northward on July 30. At the mouth of the St. Lawrence squalls, fog, and contrary winds compounded by an incompetent pilot kept the ships tacking from north to south and back again until eight transports foundered on the rocks. More than seven hundred of the British regulars, thirty-five of their women, and probably two hundred sailors were lost. General Hill called a council of war on board his ship. All the army officers wished to proceed, but Admiral Walker and the Royal Navy captains declared that the ignorance of the pilots made passage up the river impractical. Vetch offered to lead the way himself, but Walker had no stomach for the attempt. At the same time he hesitated to go home without accomplishing something. Hill, feeling no blame for the navy's reluctance, was quite ready to get back to London.

After some further delay, the British ships sailed directly for England, and the New England vessels returned to Boston. Left in the lurch once more at Lake Champlain, Nicholson tore off his wig and stamped on it in frustrated rage when he heard the news. It was no particular satisfaction to the Americans to hear later that Walker had been dismissed from the navy.

Quebec went to mass thanking God for this deliverance. At

the same time that Boston received the dread news, it suffered a disastrous fire. Helpful Increase Mather told his church members it was because they had worked on Sunday preparing Walker's expedition. A post-mortem conference of governors revealed that the colonies were too exhausted financially even to suggest a third attempt against Canada. Instead, they feared a French offensive.

A TREATY AND AN INDIAN UPRISING

In England the Tories dismissed Marlborough from command in December, 1711, and opened negotiations for peace at Utrecht, Holland. French fortunes improved, but a truce was signed in August, 1712. Louis XIV expected Acadia to be returned to him as usual. Only gradually did he relinquish this conceit. The long negotiations stopped military action in America, although the treaty was not signed until April 11, 1713. By it, England's claim to Hudson Bay was recognized, and France ceded both Acadia and Newfoundland, along with St. Kitts and Nevis in the West Indies. Spain gave up Gibraltar and Minorca to England, who had captured them. She transferred from France to England the profitable Asiento, a contract to run for thirty years permitting the sale of forty-eight hundred African slaves to the Spanish colonies per year and one trading ship annually. England recognized Philip V as king of Spain (the original alleged cause of war), and France agreed not to disturb the Protestant succession in England. Further, Louis had to renounce the French throne for his grandson, thus assuring the continued separation of the crowns of Spain and France.

The Treaty of Utrecht prevented France from upsetting the balance of power in the New World but tipped the scale somewhat in favor of England. The advantage to the American

73

colonies was that the border of Canada had been flattened. Indian raids from Maine would be discouraged by a British garrison at Annapolis Royal. New England fishermen were safe on the Grand Banks, and the fur trade of Hudson Bay could proceed unmolested. The Iroquois were recognized as English subjects, by the French if not by themselves. The flaw in all these arrangements was that France retained Cape Breton Island, just off Nova Scotia, commanding the best entrance to the St. Lawrence. Immediately she began building a new fort at a spot named Louisbourg, to which the Acadians were urged to migrate. A new threat to New England loomed, much like old Port Royal.

Queen Anne's War legally had lasted for eleven years, compared to eight for the previous war, but several years had been largely inactive. After the Haverhill raid in 1708, the only actions were the easy capture of Port Royal in 1710 and the abortive attempt toward Quebec the next year. It was a spasmodic, half-hearted sort of war. The Canadians and Floridanos seemed reluctant to commit themselves, especially without help from home, while New England's aggressive plans repeatedly went awry. For these reasons, plus the neutrality of New York, casualties were relatively light. Spaniards and Canadians together could not count more than fifty or sixty killed in action. New England suffered perhaps two hundred deaths in battles and captivity marches; in the Carolinas about one hundred and fifty had been killed so far. (It was England, of course, that lost the nine hundred soldiers and sailors on the rocks of the St. Lawrence shore, and other hundreds at Guadeloupe.) Again it was the Indians who suffered. The shooting, enslavement, or forced removal of several southern tribes was devastating. The Canadian Indians of the Northeast lost some warriors in raids on New England, perhaps fifty. Only the canny Iroquois kept clear of death in the white man's war, and in the end they won a new adherent to the league.

Intercolonial co-operation had been practiced again, but co-operation from England had proved disillusioning. At a time when several colonies were uniting in a common effort, with increasing self-confidence, they were acquiring a common disgust with their home government. This attitude was a costly one to allow to remain uncorrected. The Americans were not interested in maintaining a balance of power in Europe or in the New World. They wanted English supremacy as a step toward ousting France from North America. As positions stood, now the French were more than likely to develop their hold on the interior valleys and rivers.

Indian trouble in the South was not ended. Irritated by vicious traders and the establishment of a new colony of Swiss at New Bern, the Tuscaroras had risen against the northern Carolinians in September, 1711, and killed about a hundred and thirty. A wealthy Irish planter, Colonel John Barnwell, with thirty-three militia and five hundred Yamasees and Catawbas, struck back at the Tuscaroras and defeated them. They kept a sullen peace for two years and then were fighting again. Colonel James Moore, Jr., of South Carolina marched against them in March, 1713, with about a hundred militia and eight hundred Cherokees, Catawbas, and Creeks. He killed eight hundred warriors, while suffering only fifty-eight killed and eighty-four wounded. This defeat so overwhelmed the Tuscaroras that they began moving up to New York in waves, seeking protection among their ancient brethren. The Oneidas adopted and domiciled them, but the Iroquois never quite granted them equal status.

Hardly had the Carolinians recovered from this eruption before the Yamasees rose. They had ten towns north of Port Royal Island in a well-defined reservation, north of modern Savannah. Not only were whites encroaching, but the Carolina traders were unbelievably lawless, brutal, and cheating. The uprising may have been fomented by the neighboring Creeks, but the murderous sweep of the Yamasees in April, 1715, caught ninety traders and their families and scores of planters who lost houses and cattle and even their lives. The Creeks followed suit and wiped out the trading post in their town near modern Macon, Georgia. Governor Charles Craven and Colonel Barnwell led militia and friendly Indians against the Yamasees and defeated them. To escape further death or enslavement they fled to Florida. Some Catawbas and Apalachees then took up the hatchet and destroyed several plantation houses before they were beaten off. The Lower Creeks were frightened by now into moving closer to the French at Mobile, but the wavering Cherokees remained loyal to the English. Had they revolted too, Charleston might well have been wiped out; as it was, many Carolinians lost their lives. One result of the two brief wars was the strengthening of Spanish and French influence among the southern tribes. The Carolinians now warned London of the French peril and clamored for interior forts.

IV

American Troops under
British and American Officers

The first two clashes of colonial powers were essentially one prolonged conflict from 1689 to 1713, interrupted by a truce. The fighting stopped in 1697 because it was no longer going well for France in Europe or America. At that time Louis XIV had almost achieved the "natural boundaries" he had long sought for France—the Pyrenees, the Alps, and the Rhine. Then the foreseeable death of Charles II of Spain inspired him to essay some king-making by devious diplomacy. His duplicity provoked a second war, a war he fought not to enlarge or safeguard France but for dynastic ambition.

He failed and the cost was high. The Treaty of Utrecht prevented a family alliance of France and Spain, and soon young Philip was turning away from the country of his birth. Further, the war had bled France of immense treasure, set back her commerce, and deprived her of a piece of Canada. Third, Louis' aggrandizement had by now thoroughly aroused Europe's fears to the point where every country was interested in some combination of power to contain or reduce France. She was, in short, worse off, in 1713 than in 1667. Silently and unknowingly, under a monarch more ambitious than discerning, France had passed her peak of glory. The long reign of the Sun King was setting in national exhaustion.

When Louis XIV died in 1715, after a reign of sixty-three years, France desperately needed a prudent and progressive ruler. But Louis had outlived both of his sons and one grandson; he was succeeded by a five-year-old great-grandson. For twelve years little Louis XV was under the influence of a regent who set him an example of debauchery and uncertain diplomatic maneuvering. The regent was succeeded by Cardinal Fleury, who for seventeen years tried to restore sound financial practices while drawing closer to Spain in order to check England's growing strength. Without major reforms in the monarchy, Fleury was limited in what he could do.

The eighteenth century belonged to an emerging England. If she had endured less glamorous monarchs than France, she had enjoyed more stolid ones. More important, she was prospering from a tremendous surge of trade and she had moved politically—as France had not—from a divine-right monarchy through parliamentary supremacy to the inauguration of a two-party system of cabinet government. The cabinet was composed of the leaders of the large Privy Council who belonged to the majority party in the House of Commons. Reforms could be enacted, and a foolish monarch could be restrained from damaging the country, as he could not be in

France or Spain. England had entered the modern world politically, while France suffered perpetuation of an outmoded and inelastic form of government unequal to the burdens of empire or even of nation.

Queen Anne died in 1714, to be succeeded by a phlegmatic Hanoverian who spoke no English and disliked Britain. By his lazy indifference George I did no harm and by his dependence on others he inadvertently strengthened responsible government and the Whig ministers. Parliament's efforts to regulate the commerce of the colonies created increasing dissatisfaction in America, and prudently the ministry did not enforce the most objectionable tariffs on foreign trade.

Spain's decline continued. Victimized by inept officials, held rigid by her faith, then gnawed by her rivals in empire, she could not revitalize her traditions. Linked to an authoritarian church that upheld the incompetent aristocratic rule which supported it, Spain stifled not only liberal thought but the growth of a merchant and farming middle class that might have saved her from obsolescence. Her tightly governed colonies stayed with her, but there was strength only for defensive measures or parrying blows.

The rise of England, the drift of France, and the impotence of Spain were reflected in North America. Despite two wars the English colonies had grown impressively. From a population of two hundred thousand in 1689 they had expanded to four hundred thousand in 1715. Moreover, the migrating generation, with its memories of life in England, had largely passed on. New generations, bred in America, retained only their parents' sense of mission in migrating to the New World. The feeling that the American wilderness had been reserved for a special divine purpose was accompanied by an increasing sense of power. Risk was accepted, society was fluid even though layered, confidence in the future and in material rewards of virtue was manifest. These people were at home in their rude environment and saw themselves destined to conquer. Foreigners were adding their talents: Scots had flooded into Carolina and the middle colonies, along with some Swiss; Germans had begun to swarm toward Pennsylvania; French Huguenots came in groups to Carolina, New York, and Massachusetts. For ambitious Europeans, English America had begun to exercise its magnetic charms of opportunity, space, land, and relative civil freedom.

New France remained an exclusive, centralized corporation. Life was not too much better than in old France, and the chief differences were unattractive: a harsher climate and savage neighbors. The population increased from thirteen thousand in 1689 to no more than twenty-five thousand by 1715, despite recruitment of emigrants. The French Canadians never forgot that they were Frenchmen abroad. Many had come to make money and then return home. There were no dissenters from the Catholic faith. Social stratification lacked the extremes of wealth and poverty found in the old country, but the in-between layers were still hard and difficult to penetrate. Government was insulated from the governed, occupations were limited, few incentives stirred individual effort, and new settlements must be approved and planned in Paris.

Spanish Florida stood almost still, its white inhabitants numbering fewer than two thousand, including troops. Hazardous and continual hard work was necessary just to obtain bare nourishment. Royal officials were stumped to make recommendations that would attract settlers. "Only the great wisdom

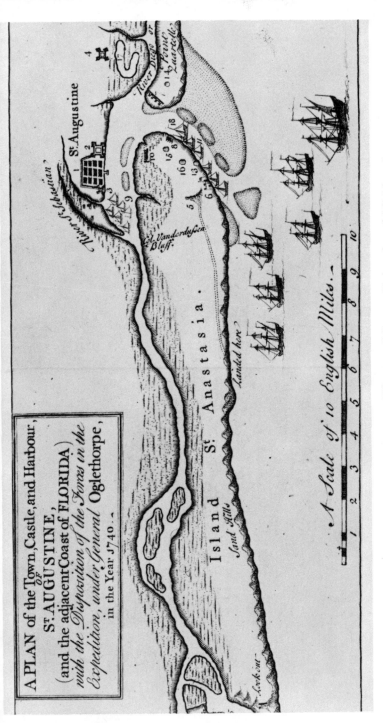

St. Augustine, Florida, in 1740. (Clements Library, University of Michigan.)

of Your Majesty," they reported in 1706, "can find and provide the solution."

Although European diplomacy veered in confusing turns, France and England remained legally at peace for more than thirty years. Not so France and Spain, or England and Spain. Louis XIV had granted to one Antoine Crozat an exclusive monopoly of the Indian trade in Louisiana for fifteen years. Crozat appointed Cadillac governor in 1712 with Bienville in command of the troops, which the king still paid. To enlarge the trade, Cadillac built a post at Natchitoches on the Red River and Fort Toulouse among the Alabamas in 1713. The latter was at the confluence of the Coosa and Tallapoosa rivers (modern Montgomery) and was considered to be the eastern bulwark of Louisiana against the English at the same time that it attracted the trade of the Upper Creeks. Next, Fort Roselie was constructed up the Mississippi among the Natchez in 1714 (modern Natchez, Mississippi).

Trouble with the Natchez two years later led to removal of Cadillac by Crozat, who in turn gave up his charter to the expensive colony in 1717. Bienville was appointed governor in 1718 by the successor Compagnie des Indes and furnished with more troops. He promptly established a new settlement on the Mississippi and named it New Orleans. The company made it the capital. Then the French started to build a fort near the mouth of the Apalachicola River, more than a hundred miles *east* of Pensacola, but desisted after Spanish protests. The quarrel with Spain led to the capture of Pensacola in 1719, but a squadron from Havana quickly reoccupied it. A French fleet came into Mobile and was used immediately to retake Pensacola.

One other distant clash checked Spain. In the summer of

1720 an expedition of one hundred and ten Spaniards and Indians under Pedro de Villasur set out northward from New Mexico to make a reconnaissance. At the forks of the North and South Platte rivers in western Nebraska, Villasur was attacked by Pawnees and French traders. He suffered twenty-six soldiers and twenty-one Indians killed, including himself. As a result expansionist ideas were given up, and Spanish dominion in the Southwest was limited to the area of Texas westward to modern California.

The war was soon over, and in the treaty of 1721 Pensacola was restored to Spain. Thereafter the French and Spanish began to think together to block the English, formally allying themselves in 1733. Meanwhile, up in the Illinois country Fort de Chartres rose on the bank of the middle Mississippi in 1721. Now Louisiana had a population of six thousand, six hundred of them Negroes.

All this activity on the part of the French had alarmed the Carolinians. Dissatisfied with their proprietary government, Carolina sent a commission to England under Colonel John Barnwell to seek royal patronage, and to persuade the Lords of Trade, first, that France was encroaching on the trade and boundaries of the southern colony and, second, that French aggression could be checked only by adopting their stratagem of frontier forts. Declaring that the French even pretended a right to commerce along the Altamaha River (across central Georgia), Barnwell argued for a string of forts starting with one on that river. Such forts would also become centers of settlement.

The Lords of Trade accepted the argument and recommended the new policy to the Privy Council. Accordingly a fort was authorized in 1721, and old General Francis Nicholson was sent over as the new royal governor with a company of regulars. Barnwell assumed that these regulars would build the fort, but actually they were one hundred invalids unable to do more than wear their uniforms. Carolina had to build the fort with its own men under the direction of Colonel Barnwell. Fort King George, near the mouth of the Altamaha (just east of Darien, Georgia, where there had been a Spanish mission), was simply a blockhouse of cypress planks, a barracks, and several huts. It was then garrisoned by the infirm and inactive company.

It was the Spanish rather than the French who claimed the Altamaha River, and Florida reacted at once. In March, 1722, a diplomatic mission arrived in Charleston to protest the new fort on Spanish land, to arrange the return of prisoners taken in Indian raids, and to determine the exact boundary between the two provinces. Governor Nicholson procrastinated by declaring that he had no power to negotiate and certainly would not abandon the fort. He wrote to the Lords of Trade, who in turn advised the king that the fort was within the charter boundaries of Carolina. England had no sound evidence actually, but sought to throw the burden of proof on Spain, on the assumption that she probably could not argue a conclusive case either.

Nevertheless, Florida persistently sent other missions to Charleston while protests were lodged in London. Finally in 1724 George I agreed to permit a conference of the Carolina and Florida governors, but delayed so long in instructing the former that the meeting initiated by the Spaniards the next year was abortive. Spain then allowed the issue to die down. More serious complaints were growing, and early in 1727 Spain declared war on both England and France and tried to take Gibraltar. Hostilities lasted only a few months. One result was that Carolina so feared the Creeks, especially a threatened attack on Port Royal, that the garrison at Fort King George was withdrawn to that town. At the same time the Spanish-backed Yamasees were encouraged to ravage outlying Carolina plantations. Carolina organized a punitive expedition of two hundred whites and Indians under Colonel John Palmer in March, 1728. The three remaining Yamasee villages were close to St. Augustine. Palmer attacked one, killed thirty warriors, captured fifteen, wounded others, and when the survivors fled into the Spanish fort he burned the village. This aggressiveness subdued the war spirit of the neighboring Creeks.

In the area of Maine the French of Canada and the English were having trouble that reached a bloody climax before it quieted down. The basic difficulty was the vagueness of the boundaries of Acadia. While the French controlled it, the region included modern Nova Scotia, New Brunswick, and the northeastern part of Maine down to the Kennebec River. After the cession to Great Britain, France said Acadia meant only the Nova Scotia peninsula. Be that as it may, France kept the allegiance of the Abenakis, and Father Sebastien Rale, Jesuit missionary, lived at their village of Norridgewock on the Kennebec. As English settlers pushed their way up to the Kennebec, Father Rale fanned the resentment of the Norridgewock Abenakis. In a council with them he was abetted by the bad manners of Governor Samuel Shute of Massachusetts. Tension grew, and Indians burned Georgetown at the mouth of the Kennebec. Governor Vaudreuil furnished them with powder. Other raids occurred, and Massachusetts sent Colonel Thomas Westbrook and three hundred men to seize Rale, but they were unsuccessful.

The Indians next burned Brunswick. Governor Shute and council declared war against the Abenakis in July, 1722. The lower house insisted on running the war if it was to be carried on, and by this quarrelsome delay Colonel Westbrook did not strike the Indians until February, 1723, when he burned a village above modern Bangor.

In August, 1724, another English expedition struck at Norridgewock, killing twenty-eight Indians and Father Rale, who was fighting with them. Governor Vaudreuil now directed the Abenakis against western Massachusetts as a diversionary tactic. For protection Massachusetts built Fort Dummer (near Brattleboro, Vermont). Early the next year a company of men under Captain John Lovewell set out northward from Dunstable and brought back ten scalps. Encouraged, Captain Lovewell took out a party of thirty-four in April toward the White Mountains. They fell into an ambush, and Lovewell, with eight others, was killed. The remainder pulled back, fighting all day. Only fourteen returned home. Finally in 1726 various Abenaki chiefs met with Massachusetts commissioners at Casco Bay and made peace.

New York took warning, and Governor William Burnet ordered the building of a fortified trading post at Oswego, on the shore of Lake Ontario, in 1728. It was an effort to attract the canoes of fur-trading Indians from entering the St. Lawrence. Three years later France boldly pushed down into New York and started Fort St. Frédéric at Crown Point, near the southern end of Lake Champlain.

On the lower Mississippi the French suffered a paralyzing blow. In a sudden revolt the Natchez destroyed Fort Roselie late in 1729 and killed two hundred and fifty men, taking their women and children prisoners. The commandant was blamed for his arrogant demands and injustices. The French retaliated immediately from New Orleans and rescued the women and children, but the Natchez escaped. The fort was rebuilt. The next year Governor Périer himself led a thousand soldiers and Indians against the Natchez. He captured four hundred and twenty-seven of them and sold them to San Domingo as slaves. The remnant Natchez were adopted into the neighboring Chickasaw nation. But the expenses of this war were so great that the Compagnie des Indes surrendered its charter, and Louisiana became a royal colony like Canada.

Bienville, who had been called home in 1724, was returned as governor early in 1733. Unwilling to let matters rest, he demanded that the Chickasaws give up the Natchez they were protecting, and when they refused he made war on them. He ordered Pierre d'Artaguiette, commandant at Fort de Chartres, to gather troops and join him. In 1736 he attacked the Chickasaws in modern northern Mississippi and was repelled with a loss of about one hundred and thirty soldiers. Returning to New Orleans, he left D'Artaguiette to be defeated and killed along with nineteen other Frenchmen, including the Sieur de Vincennes, who had founded a post on the Wabash River named for himself. Bienville called for more troops from France, and after they arrived he assembled a force of twelve hundred in 1738 and marched up the Mississippi. Fort L'Assomption (near modern Memphis) was established in 1739, and when in fearful anticipation the Chickasaws sued for peace, it was granted.

In the midst of these Indian raids and border clashes, England created another colony below South Carolina. In 1732 the government granted land for a period of twenty-one years to a board of philanthropic gentlemen interested in relieving debtors. The new colony, called Georgia, would also check Spanish ambitions. It had been promoted by South Carolina to serve as a buffer against Spanish-dominated Indians. Georgia was to extend from the Savannah River south to the Altamaha, and as far west as the Pacific. No governor or assembly was permitted.

James Oglethorpe, a thirty-six-year-old army officer, was the moving spirit in the enterprise and the infant colony's protector. He had been a member of Parliament for a decade, concerned with relief of English debtors. To him and his friends an asylum for debtors in America, with opportunity for a fresh start, appeared much more sensible and humane than imprisonment at home. To encourage their rehabilitation the trustees had provided almost communal ownership of land and forbidden the importation of liquor and slaves. Debtors, it turned out, were not attracted to a place menaced by fevers, Indians, and Spaniards, while the need to attract settlers forced the trustees ultimately to abandon their prohibitions and allow immediate private ownership of land.

Oglethorpe was notably successful in making an alliance with the powerful Creeks, although he was oddly indifferent to his southern boundary. After founding the town of Savannah with one hundred and twenty colonists, he explored southward beyond the Altamaha and decided in 1736 to build Fort Fredericka on St. Simon's Island (where there had been a Spanish mission), followed by two more forts on Cumberland Island, and another on San Juan Island near the mouth of St. Johns River. He also founded Fort Augusta, 125 miles up the Savannah. Some Scot Highlanders were enlisted and sent over as defense protection.

The Spaniards, who had formed a new family compact with France when Georgia was settled, protested vigorously against this new and more dangerous encroachment. Yet Oglethorpe and Governor Francisco Sanchez reached an agreement in 1736 about their common boundary and referred it home to London and Madrid. For his concessions, Sanchez was called home and hanged. For his achievement, Oglethorpe was given a regiment of new recruits and made commander of forces in both Georgia and South Carolina. Florida was disturbed, and the home governments finally provided for adjudicating the border and other issues, pending which the Altamaha should remain the line. The chief other issue was Spain's searching of British ships suspected of illegal trading with the Spanish colonies. The ministry of Robert Walpole, however, was dedicated to peace.

It was then, in the spring of 1738, that ship's Captain Robert Jenkins opened his handkerchief before a Parliamentary committee and displayed his severed ear—which apparently he had been carrying around with him fondly for seven years. The old Asiento of 1713 had allowed Britons to sell slaves in the Spanish West Indies and *one* shipload of trade goods per year. Inevitably British merchants exceeded this limitation by bribing Spanish customs officials. To help keep the trade in line the two countries had agreed on the mutual right to search each other's ships for contraband goods. Captain Jenkins was not a slaver but an Asiento smuggler. In 1731 he had been caught by the Spaniards and punished by having one ear cut off. Why he had kept quiet all this time may be surmised. Spain's high-handed and cruel methods of search and seizure had inflamed public resentment to such a pitch that Captain Jenkins could now tell his story and become a popular hero. When asked what he did at the moment of mutilation, Jenkins answered: "I commended my soul to God, and my cause to my country!"

The statement aroused the nation to a war fever. Cries of "No search!" filled the air, and the House of Lords passed a

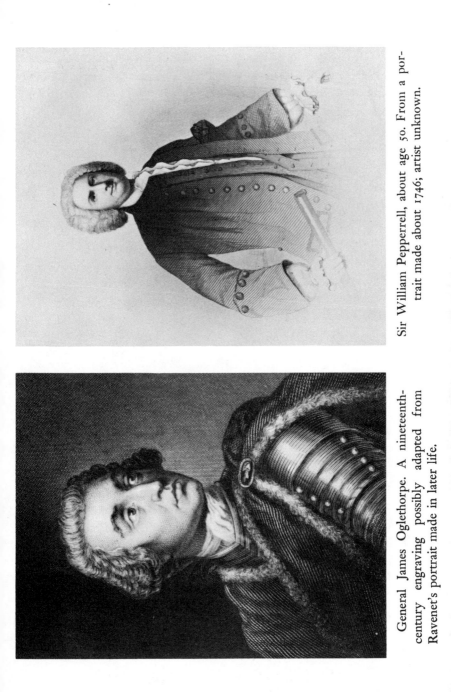

General James Oglethorpe. A nineteenth-century engraving possibly adapted from Ravenet's portrait made in later life.

Sir William Pepperrell, about age 50. From a portrait made about 1746; artist unknown.

resolution denying the right which the government had granted by treaty. Walpole was forced to remonstrate, and in January, 1739, Spain agreed to pay £95,000 damages to English merchants. But as nothing was said about punishing Spanish captains or abrogating the right of search, the offer was denounced. For the first time in Parliament a cutting voice of scathing opposition was heard—that of young William Pitt. Walpole knew he must resign or appease the nation by declaring war. He took the latter course in October, 1739.

As soon as word reached America, General Oglethorpe gathered some troops and Indians and on December 1 embarked for St. Johns River. He captured two small forts and seventy prisoners, and by controlling the river cut off St. Augustine's communication with Apalachee. His limited purpose accomplished, Oglethorpe returned to Fort Fredericka and then visited South Carolina to mature his plans for an attack on St. Augustine. By May, 1740, he had rounded up five hundred Indians, four hundred South Carolina militia under Colonel Alexander Vander Deusen, five hundred troops from his own regiment, plus four hundred Rangers and Scot Highlanders. It was to be an attack co-ordinated with British naval vessels.

Under Governor Manuel de Montiano, Fort San Marcos at St. Augustine had been enlarged and much strengthened. Fifty cannon looked out over high stone walls. With the news of war, entrenchments were thrown up around the town and connecting to the fort. The garrison now amounted to about eleven hundred, and the rest of the inhabitants numbered about a thousand.

After some delay Oglethorpe approached St. Augustine and captured an outlying post, Fort San Diego, containing fifty-seven men. Another one, Fort Moosa, only two miles from the capital, was evacuated without resistance. Ordering his naval squadron to block two passages into St. Augustine, Oglethorpe led his land forces to the rear of the town for a simultaneous assault from east and west. Unfortunately, the English ships could not stand in close enough to bombard the town, while the light Spanish galleys, just beyond cannon range, could fire on any landing parties. Oglethorpe had no choice but to lay siege on June 13. He hoped to draw out some of the Spaniards by detaching a party of forty Indians and eighty-five whites under Colonel Palmer to show themselves but to keep continuously on the move. Attracted by the comforts of deserted Fort Moosa, Palmer's men insisted on sleeping there three nights running. On June 15 before dawn the Spaniards surprised the party, killed fifty whites and Indians, and took twenty soldiers prisoner. But the Spaniards reputedly lost one hundred and thirty-two men in the attack.

Oglethorpe stepped up his cannonading of Fort San Marcos for twenty days but did little damage. The real danger faced by the Spaniards was starvation, until three small ships laden with provisions from Cuba gained the inland passage from the south and relieved the fort. Oglethorpe was correspondingly discouraged. Temperamentally unsuited to siege operations, the Indians were impatient to depart. The Carolina militia was both deserting and falling ill. The hurricane season drew near. Realizing his cannon were too small for the stone walls of the fort, and his ships too large to maintain a blockade or carry the naval guns closer, Oglethorpe raised the siege on July 10. His total losses were a few more than fifty killed, about as many wounded, and twenty captured. The Spaniards had lost perhaps two hundred killed and captured.

Troops under British and American Officers

If the enemy was deterred from taking the offensive for two years, Oglethorpe was less fortunate among his neighbors. The disappointed South Carolinians blamed him for the failure of the expedition and extolled Colonel Vander Deusen over him. While Oglethorpe was depressed by this calumny, the focus of war shifted to the Caribbean.

Admiral Edward Vernon, who had captured Porto Bello, Panama, was now dispatched to take Cartagena, Colombia's seaport. Land forces were recruited in America as well as in England, and thirty-five hundred Americans were sought. They were to be enrolled as an American regiment on the British establishment, with all captains, ensigns, and half the lieutenants to be Americans. Colonial assemblies had only to feed the troops and transport them to the West Indies. A force of nine thousand was assembled at Jamaica under command of Brigadier General Thomas Wentworth, who hid his incompetence under slowness. Vernon carried them to Cartagena on March 3, 1741, and urged Wentworth to strike at once. The latter got part of his troops and supplies ashore and opened fire on the town three weeks later. When he finally ordered an assault he met with staggering butchery. Soon the rains came and then yellow fever. Vernon re-embarked the decimated forces on April 17. The expedition tried to redeem itself in Cuba but only wasted months. No more than six hundred Americans survived!

In the colonies the effect of this debacle must have been embittering, for clearly the lives lost were the direct result of bungling by the British command. Not much comment can be found, but surely the Americans did not easily forget this fatal co-operation with British professionals. A weary Virginia captain named Lawrence Washington, who returned broken in health, named his Potomac River plantation after the admiral—Mount Vernon.

France had not jumped to Spain's defense, because she actually believed in the freedom of the seas as England did, in opposition to Spain's arrogant effort to make the Caribbean and Gulf of Mexico Spanish waters. But France as well as other European countries were being sucked into the vortex of war. Late in October, 1740, Emperor Charles VI had died and left Austria to his daughter, Maria Theresa. Male Hapsburgs resented her, and Frederick of Prussia claimed the Austrian province of Silesia and set out to seize it. He found allies in Spain, France, Bavaria, and Saxony. England favored Austria, and Walpole resigned early in 1742. The new ministry, hot for war, loaned money to Queen Maria Theresa, subsidized Hanoverian and Hessian troops to help her, and finally landed an English army in Holland.

Spain and France now agreed on their own objectives. They would fight to recover Gibraltar and Minorca for Spain, to destroy Georgia, and to transfer the Asiento from England to France. The latter also expected to pick up the Austrian Netherlands (modern Belgium) as her prize. The burden of a new offensive in America rested on Spain. It was not until May, 1742, that Cuba was able to send a fleet and about three thousand men to St. Augustine for an attack on Georgia and the Carolinas. As soon as word reached Oglethorpe, he appealed to South Carolina for troops but was refused. Late in June the first Spanish ships appeared off Cumberland Island, but the energetic general took to his boats and drove them off, saving Fort William. It was only a preliminary encounter.

A week later a large squadron was sighted off St. Simon's

Island headed for the river on which Fort Fredericka stood. Georgia's handful of ships disputed the passage and killed seventeen of the enemy troops before giving way. The Spaniards landed four miles south of the fort and discharged more than three thousand men. They were actually two armies: Cuban troops under Don Antonio Arredondo, and a few more than six hundred Florida troops under Governor de Montiano. Included in the former was a regiment of artillery, a regiment of Negroes, and a regiment of mulattoes. Oglethorpe commanded only six hundred and fifty men, including Indians and militia. He dispatched another appeal to Charleston, imploring help from Royal Navy ships that preferred to chase Spanish prizes.

When a reconnaissance force approached Fort Fredericka, Oglethorpe hastened out to meet them in the woods. Suddenly attacked, the Spanish advance of one hundred and twenty-five woodsmen and forty-five Indians were almost all killed or captured. Pursuit of several miles brought the Georgians into collision with a second party of three hundred Spaniards under Captain Barba. Part of the English force was routed, but a company of Rangers and a platoon of Highlanders passed through some woods and gained the rear of the Spaniards. Soon the Spaniards returned, stacked their arms, and sat down to rest. The Georgians now fell on them, killing one hundred and sixty-seven, including the commander, and taking twenty prisoners. Oglethorpe came up with reinforcements in time to chase the survivors.

This double defeat produced ill feelings in the Spanish camp. The Cuban forces refused to do duty with the Floridanos, and the regiment of dragoons separated from both. The commodore called the marines aboard ship. Oglethorpe was not long in learning of these quarrels and decided to strike with five hundred of his men on the night of July 12. They marched close to the Spanish camp, but withdrew when a Frenchman deserted to the enemy. He was actually a spy for Governor de Montiano. Oglethorpe paused in fear of an attack, since the Spaniards would learn how small a force he actually had. Wondering how to counteract the Frenchman's treachery, he finally composed a letter in French. Then he released a Spanish prisoner and gave him money to deliver the letter secretly to the Frenchman.

As expected, when the prisoner returned to camp he was taken before De Montiano for questioning. He said nothing about the letter until it was found on him. Then he confessed that he had been paid to deliver it to the French spy. The governor read the letter. The writer said he had received the "reward money" for the recipient and that if the latter could now lead the Spanish boats farther up the river where the "hidden batteries" were, his reward would be doubled. If he could not do that, he should try to keep the Spaniards on the island three more days, because word had just come that two thousand men and six ships were on their way from Charleston. Also, he should be careful to make no mention that Admiral Vernon was preparing to descend on St. Augustine.

This devilish stratagem disturbed De Montiano. He questioned the Frenchman, who denied the lies, of course, but the governor could not be sure but what his man was a double spy. He called a council of war. A minority viewed the letter as a fiction designed to save Fort Fredericka from attack; but the majority distrusted the Frenchman under the circumstances and believed in the genuineness of the letter. While they argued, word was brought in that three sail were seen off the end of the island. Here were the Charleston warships! The Spaniards hurried to embark leaving cannon, supplies, and even unburied dead. The Cubans were only too glad to escape further maneuvering with the despised Floridanos. Suddenly the threat to Georgia evaporated on the horizon.

When the truth was known about the meagerness of Oglethorpe's defending forces and lack of reinforcements, Governor de Montiano was censured, and Arredondo was thrown into Havana's jail. Oglethorpe was hailed throughout the colonies. The year expired without new offensives. In March, 1743, Oglethorpe attacked St. Augustine again. His Indians killed more than forty of a Spanish party. He carried no heavy cannon with him and apparently expected to lure the Spaniards out of their sheltering fort. They would not come out. All that Oglethorpe could do was lay waste the surrounding country and go back home. Spain felt unequal to mounting a new offensive, and the destruction of Georgia was laid aside. Oglethorpe returned to England in September, 1743, partly to answer petty charges by a disgruntled officer in his regiment and mainly to impress on Parliament the necessity of defending Georgia as the bulwark of the southern colonies.

He found that war with Spain was overshadowed by the emergence of France once more as the chief enemy of England. Cardinal Fleury died, and the unpredictable Louis XV was dominated by successive mistresses. King George II, leading his troops into Holland, was suddenly attacked by a French army late in June, 1743, although the two countries were, while ranged on opposite sides of the Austrian quarrel, legally at peace. The English fought their way out of this trap, and the Battle of Dettingen is remembered as the last time a British monarch appeared at the head of his army. The clash drove both countries to declare war on each other in March, 1744.

It was the War of the Austrian Succession, in America called King George's War. ~~March 1742~~

Oglethorpe never returned to America. He served at home in the new war. By seniority he moved up steadily in the army to the rank of full general. Though his interest in Georgia moderated after it became a royal colony, he remained sympathetic to colonial aspirations. He lived into his eighty-ninth year—long enough to welcome John Adams to London in 1785 as the first United States minister to the Court of St. James's.

V

Militia and the Royal Navy
King George's War

News of the double declaration of war by France and England reached the English colonies in the normal time of two months—late in May, 1744. But the news had carried to Cape Breton Island somewhat earlier, and the French acted promptly. On May 14 the military governor ordered Captain François Duvivier with six hundred men to sail from Louisbourg down the coast, across the strait separating the island from Nova Scotia and capture the English fishing village of Canseau. It was safeguarded by a wooden redoubt and a garrison of about eighty men. Completely surprised, the troops surrendered on condition that they be sent to Boston. For the time being, however, the prisoners were ferried back to Louisbourg—a fatal error of judgment on the part of the French commander in view of the Boston destination.

The easy success of this stroke led the French into a second mistake—an attempt against Annapolis Royal, the old Port Royal. Captain Duvivier was again directed to command the expedition at the beginning of summer. The English fortification was in poor shape, but tenable by determined men. The garrison numbered about a hundred effectives under Major Paul Mascarene, a very determined son of a Huguenot refugee. He refused Duvivier's summons to surrender. As the Frenchman was expecting two warships with two hundred and fifty regulars in a matter of hours, he postponed any assault, while the English strengthened their position. The expected French vessels reached Louisbourg, but their captains refused to sail on to Annapolis without orders from Paris. Gradually Duvivier gave up hope of reinforcements and called on the old French Acadians to join him. Remembering the evils of openly taking sides, they refused, agreeing only to build scaling ladders. Duvivier made a few half-hearted attacks but did not use the ladders. Then to his dismay a ship from Boston entered the harbor with reinforcements for Major Mascarene. Giving up too easily, Duvivier sailed back to Louisbourg. His feeble attempt, however, had demonstrated how much at the mercy of the Louisbourg French were fishing opportunities of New Englanders.

Now, after all the delay, the English prisoners of Canseau were transported to Boston. They had all seen the physical conditions of Louisbourg, its walls and batteries, and Lieutenant John Bradstreet reported them to Governor William Shirley, urging that the island be captured. He may not have originated the proposal even so, because William Vaughan, Harvard 1722 and a merchant in fish and timber on the Maine coast, had long been hostile to Louisbourg and he too advised

Governor Shirley to attack it with militia. Many merchants and fishermen of Massachusetts were aroused by the near escape of Annapolis Royal from capture.

Not as yet known to the Americans, the voice of a London merchant had been raised against Cape Breton Island. In January, 1745, he proposed to the ministry that New England troops and Royal Navy vessels should make a joint descent on Cape Breton in the spring, because the island was needed to protect the valuable English fishing rights.

The Louisbourg fortification had been started in 1720 after plans of Vauban and required twenty years to complete. It was called the "Gibraltar of the New World" and was the only French naval station on the American coast. Stone walls thirty feet high supported 250 cannon on the ramparts. As well as guarding the main entrance to the St. Lawrence, it was a haven for French privateers in time of war. Besides the fortified town on the west side of the harbor, there were two separated batteries: one on an island in the harbor entrance, and the other, the Grand Battery, inside the harbor on its north center shore. The layout was such that if an attacking squadron got past the island battery it would come under the guns of the Grand Battery and of the fort itself.

What Lieutenant Bradstreet pointed out was that the garrison was small—six hundred discontented regulars, which number might be tripled by militia; that cannon was lacking, there being fewer than a hundred in place; that there were higher hills west of the town; and finally that the wall of the Grand Battery had two breaches not repaired.

Governor Shirley was won over. Born in England, he was appointed governor in 1741 after a decade of law practice in Boston, where he learned to handle the ambitious merchants

99

and touchy Puritans with skill. Fifty years old, he stood six feet tall and was heavy, and he lived soberly with his energetic wife and eight children. Early in January, 1745, he appeared before the Massachusetts court and asked the members to take an oath of secrecy concerning his message. They consented to this novel demand and then heard him propose a Massachusetts expedition against Louisbourg. A committee of both houses considered the matter for several days and then the court voted it down. By this time the secret had leaked out, and Boston merchants busied themselves arousing support for the governor's bold plan. They petitioned the court for a reconsideration, and the proposal was approved.

Shirley had written to England asking for naval support from Commodore Peter Warren in the West Indies. He also issued a call for help from neighboring colonies as far south as Pennsylvania. All kinds of shipping would be needed. Command of the expedition was given to William Pepperrell, forty-nine-year-old president of the Massachusetts Council, militia colonel, and a prosperous merchant of Kittery in Maine. He was distinguished for good sense rather than for military experience. He was also popular, a primary requisite.

As men and ships assembled in Boston, the enterprise gained something of the air of a crusade in the wake of the recent religious revival. It was supported by the clergy, for was it not directed against the popish French, those instigators of devilish Indian raids? Connecticut sent five hundred men under Colonel Roger Wolcott, who was made second in command; New Hampshire contributed four hundred and fifty men under Colonel Samuel Moore. In the Massachusetts and Maine district three thousand men were raised, and both Vaughan and Bradstreet took commissions. Rhode Island sent only an armed ship.

New York gave ten cannon, 24-pounders, bringing to thirty-four the number of cannon available. Pennsylvania and New Jersey offered provisions. Altogether fifteen armed vessels and a hundred transports were made ready.

Down in Philadelphia a skeptical Benjamin Franklin wrote to his brother in Boston: "Fortified towns are hard nuts to crack; and your teeth are not accustomed to it. Taking strong places is a particular trade, which you have taken up without serving an apprenticeship to it."

Full of enthusiasm and self-confidence the expedition began embarking on March 24. A week later Governor Shirley received the encouraging word from Commodore Warren that he was on his way north with three naval ships to co-operate with the New England forces. Warren was forty-two years old and had lived in New York City (he owned Greenwich Village) since 1730; he was also married to a Delancey.

The transports began arriving in Canseau after April 1. On the twenty-third, to everyone's joy, Warren appeared in a sixty-gun ship, accompanied by three forty-gun ships. The Connecticut regiment in its own transport fleet arrived the next day. "Wee have all the help now that wee expect," one diarist concluded succinctly.

The cold weather of this latitude began to moderate, and ice melted out of rivers and harbors. Finally on April 29 the huge fleet sailed for Louisbourg and the next morning came to anchor in Gabarus Bay, west of Louisbourg harbor and three miles west of town. A token force of seventy-five Frenchmen came out to oppose the first landing boats, but the latter were only making a feint. They suddenly turned and pulled for shore a mile away, where others had preceded them. The actual landing was hardly contested. Three Americans were wounded;

three Frenchmen were killed and twelve taken; the others retreated to the town and set fire to twenty-three houses outside the walls. Bells were heard in Louisbourg calling the rural inhabitants into the safety of the fort.

Peaceful landing of the Americans continued all that day and the next, May 1. Camp was established on a small stream to the east, less than two miles from Louisbourg's walls. Some of the companies moved forward to observe the great fortress. They were seen, and cannon were fired at them without effect.

A detachment of four hundred under Lieutenant Colonel Vaughan was sent around to the north shore of the harbor to reconnoiter the Grand Battery. They set fire to some houses in the vicinity that night. Next morning, May 2, they were surprised to see no smoke issuing from the battery and no other sign of life. Cautiously they approached the two breaches in the wall which Bradstreet had noticed earlier. No one challenged them. So they walked in and took possession of the abandoned stronghold. Believing they could not hold it, the French had left it during the night after spiking the cannon. The French officers had wanted to blow up the battery, but the engineer had foolishly prevailed against them. Such was the American luck.

The Grand Battery contained thirty disabled cannon—twenty-eight of 42 pounds and two of 18—and hundreds of shot and shells. In anticipation of capturing spiked cannon, the New Englanders had brought smiths and tools for removing those spikes from the powder holes. The French in Louisbourg now tried to retrieve their mistake on May 3 by sending a force in small boats to retake the battery, but they were fought off. Then some of the Louisbourg cannon began firing on the battery. To their surprise they were answered on May 4 by

Landing of the New England troops at Louisbourg, 1745. (John Carter Brown Library, Brown University.)

three cannon which had been cleared. Several more cannon were soon put in operating condition, and since they were larger than anything the New Englanders had been able to bring along, some of them were dragged around to the American line to be used against the town.

Their luck continued when Commodore Warren captured a French supply ship bound for Louisbourg. It was loaded with bread, meat, and flour. Thus provisioned and equipped with siege guns, all from the enemy, Pepperrell sent a summons into Louisbourg to surrender. The commandant, Louis du Chambon, rejected it, of course. Pepperrell pushed forward several small batteries of light cannon to play more effectively on the walls of the fortress. Bombs were being lobbed into the town and setting fires. The French fired briskly but were at a disadvantage. Apparently a land attack from the west had never been foreseen. The French seemingly expected to meet only a naval attack by an attempt of the enemy to force his way into the harbor. The biggest battery in the fortification faced the water, and the cannon could not be swung around to fire westward. As for the island battery, the Americans were using the Grand Battery to keep it quiet.

Pepperrell kept skirmishing parties out over the island to crush resistance among the more isolated inhabitants and to take prisoners. Occasionally bloody fights developed with Indians or militia squads. Gunners and officers were also falling before exploding cannon or shells from the French. Muskets were fired steadily at any heads appearing above the walls. When a French warship appeared on the horizon, Warren pursued and captured it, winning sixty-four guns, five hundred and sixty crewmen, and a cargo of munitions.

Around to the east side of the harbor at Lighthouse Point

a new battery was prepared to fire directly on the island battery. Hauling cannon around to it was a tedious job, so two attempts were made to storm the island. The first, involving some eight hundred men on May 23, never got started, as too many showed up drunk. A council of war exonerated the officers but called for volunteers for a second attempt. About four hundred agreed to participate on the night of May 26. They made an undetected landing on the island, then some drunken fool proposed a cheer to mark their safe arrival. The noise alerted the French, who killed sixty and captured one hundred and nineteen. The others escaped, but the bungled business depressed the army.

Finally on June 10 the new battery on Lighthouse Point opened fire on the island. Louisbourg itself had endured a severe pounding, and one gate was partly demolished. Warren and Pepperrell, growing impatient with the siege, agreed to lead a joint sea and land assault. Warren made a rousing speech to the army on June 15, promising to sail his ships into the bay. Orders were given to make scaling ladders. Then about sunset a flag of truce came out of Louisbourg asking for a cessation of arms so that surrender of the town might be discussed. The next day was given over to negotiations, and on June 17 the mighty citadel was handed over to Pepperrell. Although every Frenchman was allowed to keep his personal property, they were all going to be transported to France.

Warren suggested keeping the French flag flying so as to lure French vessels toward the harbor. Several merchant ships, one loaded with gold and silver, sailed into the trap. Soon the prizes he had taken amounted to more than a million pounds sterling. Half the value went to the British Crown, and half to the naval captains; nothing went to the New England troops, who also were deprived of hoped-for booty from plundering. Complaints were made of Warren, and jealousy flared that he might claim all credit for the victory.

The French officers gave out as reasons for the capitulation their lack of men, food, and powder. It is true that they were outnumbered: about six hundred regulars plus thirteen 'hundred Frenchmen and their wives and children, against four thousand New Englanders plus a few hundred seamen. Only fifty-three French regulars were killed and eighty wounded; how many civilians were casualties is not known. As for food, undoubtedly the crowded town lacked sufficient supplies, and capture of the French provision ship was a severe blow. Whether there was a lack of powder is more questionable: after the surrender the English found one hundred and twelve barrels of gunpowder in the town and on the island. The destructiveness of the cannonade was self-evident; only one building in the town was not hit. "We gave them" Pepperrell reported, "about nine thousand cannon balls and six hundred bombs."

On the English side, Governor Shirley was informed that one hundred and one men were killed during the siege, and about thirty died of disease in camp. This figure presumably does not include about thirty-six men killed in breaking up the nine fishing settlements around Cape Breton. Fever and dysentery were so prevalent that about fifteen hundred were incapable of duty shortly before the capitulation.

Militia Colonel John Bradstreet was put in command of the captured town, and repairs were immediately started on the fortress. Ships were prepared to transport four thousand Frenchmen to France, under convoy of Commodore Warren, who had earned Pepperrell's affection not only for his vigorous co-operation but as well for his understanding of militia foibles. It was an unprecedented exhibition of joint naval and army endeavor, the more notable for the army being colonial militia, and was owing to the good sense of the two commanders. It did not occur again until 1759 at the taking of Quebec.

News of the victory set off wild celebrations in America and England. Massachusetts ministers gave full credit to the Lord, but could not escape being touched with pride over the achievement of local arms. Warren was promoted to admiral and appointed governor of Louisbourg, while Pepperrell was made a baronet (the first native American so honored) and along with Shirley was appointed colonel of a regiment of regulars to be raised in America. Neither regiment was filled up before both were dissolved. For Shirley the reward was much less than he expected.

Holding Louisbourg proved to be much more costly than taking it. The New England troops found to their annoyance that they must now garrison and repair the fortress. Camp diseases swept through their ranks, and by the spring of 1746 Shirley reported that eight hundred and ninety had died! Everyone was on edge: the troops anxious to go home to escape the epidemic and also to protect their frontiers from Indian forays, Shirley eager to promote an expedition against Quebec as quickly as possible.

Glorious as was the capture of Louisbourg, it was but a single battle and the victory had slight effect on the border between Canada and New England. The forgotten terror of Indian raids soon became a frightful reality to a new generation. Mindful of the important role that the Iroquois could play, Governor George Clinton called them to conference at Albany in June, 1744. A vice admiral, Clinton had obtained the governorship in the hope of avoiding bankruptcy. He turned out to be indolent and completely dependent on ill-chosen advisers, with the result that the New York Assembly increased its authority over the executive while the governor grew rich. Clinton was no more successful with the Iroquois; the best he could do was obtain a kind of neutrality from them: they would not help the French and neither would they help the English unless the latter were attacked and asked for help. Some chiefs agreed to accompany Massachusetts commissioners to Penobscot, Maine, to win the allegiance of the Abenaki subtribes. But they were not successful and in October Massachusetts formally took up the hatchet against the eastern tribes and posted rewards for their scalps.

New York was divided in its response to raids. A powerful faction in the Assembly was opposed to everything Governor Clinton might suggest, even at the risk of losing the border settlements. Thus the governor could not provide the defenses he wanted or support those Iroquois who were willing to fight, except by drawing on London funds. He had a strong right arm in William Johnson, a young Irish nephew of Commodore Warren, who had arrived to look after his uncle's huge landholdings along the Mohawk River. Johnson ingratiated himself with the Mohawks, was adopted, and gained great influence over them. At this time he amiably took their daughters as mistresses and after 1758 lived with Mohawk Molly Brant until his death; by her he had eight half-breed children. The New York governor appointed him colonel of the Six Nations to supervise their activities.

Massachusetts moved more decisively and despite the expense of the expedition to Louisbourg undertook to construct three forts between the Connecticut River and the New York boundary. They were Fort Pelham at modern Rowe, Fort Shirley at Heath, and Fort Massachusetts at Adams. In addition, it had to supply a garrison for Fort Number 4 up the Connecticut River at modern Charlestown, New Hampshire. The colony of New Hampshire claimed the fort as lying within its jurisdiction, then argued that since it was useful only to Massachusetts, Massachusetts should support it. In all, Massachusetts posted four hundred and forty men along its northwestern frontier.

Border warfare resumed in earnest in July, 1745, with an attack on the Great Meadow Fort (Putney, Vermont), on modern Keene, New Hampshire, and on St. George's Fort (Thomaston, Maine). New York was temporarily safe because of its Iroquois residents, whom Governor Clinton called to a second congress at Albany in October. They conceded a willingness to take up arms against the French when the governor should ask them. Yet he hesitated over bringing retaliatory raids on his province.

Toward the end of November, New York was invaded nevertheless. The Sieur de Marin and Father Picquet led three hundred Canadians and two hundred Indians against the Dutch settlement of Saratoga. The small militia garrison of twelve had been recalled because the Assembly would not spend money to make the barracks habitable. Thirty inhabitants were killed and between sixty and a hundred, most of them Negro slaves, were taken prisoner. Many houses were burned. The New York Assembly now roused itself to rebuild the fort.

The spring of 1746 brought a renewal of raids. Number 4 was attacked in April and twice in May. The settlers at Keene drove off another band of Indians. Ambushes were laid in May from Albany to Schenectady, and a dozen men were killed.

Another strong attack on Number 4 was resisted in June. This fort seemed so formidable to the French that their attention turned to Fort Massachusetts. In August, Pierre François de Rigaud, son of the old Canadian governor, Vaudreuil, led seven hundred French and Indians against the stronghold. At that moment it held but twenty-two men, three women, and five children. Further, eight of the men were sick. But the fort was under the temporary command of an iron sergeant named John Hawks. He fought back bravely against overwhelming odds until he had eleven killed, two wounded, and his powder ran low. Rigaud proposed terms. Hawks surrendered on condition that his people become prisoners of the French, not of the Indians, and be subject to exchange. Rigaud agreed. The fort was burned and the garrison was marched off toward Crown Point. Then Rigaud broke his word and gave some of the prisoners to the Indians. To their credit the savages harmed none of them and even carried the wounded and the children. The next year the captives were duly exchanged and returned to Massachusetts, except for ten who died in Canada.

Meanwhile Governor Shirley had vigorously pressed for an expedition against Quebec. His proposal was approved in England by the secretary of state, the Duke of Newcastle, who directed other colonial governors to co-operate. He also promised eight battalions of regulars under Lieutenant General James St. Clair to meet the colonial troops at Louisbourg. The smell of victory inspired heroic efforts: Massachusetts raised 3,500 men, Connecticut 1,000, New York 1,600, New Hampshire 500, Rhode Island 300, New Jersey 500, even Maryland 300 and Virginia 100. All these men were to be paid, clothed, and armed from England and they were promised booty. In addition, Parliament voted to reimburse the New England colonies for the expenses of capturing Louisbourg. Canada grew thoroughly frightened by rumors of the coming juggernaut. The militia were ready in July, 1746, but the British regulars did not appear. In fact, they never came, being used instead on an abortive expedition to the French coast. Shades of 1709! Newcastle did not deign to explain until the following spring. The colonial troops were dismissed.

Failing in this direction, Shirley directed fifteen hundred of his militia to join New York troops in an attempt on Fort St. Frédèric at Crown Point. Even this secondary objective had to be abandoned by Shirley's recall of the troops upon receipt of alarming intelligence from Nova Scotia of a French fleet ready to seize Louisbourg and burn Boston.

France had not accepted the loss of Louisbourg as final. A fleet of sixty-five ships and more than thirty-one hundred troops were gathered at Brest under command of the Duc d'Enville. It sailed in June, 1746, for the Azores, where a storm wrecked one ship and a mysterious pestilence broke out. In September as the fleet came in sight of Nova Scotia it was battered by a hurricane before making Chibucto Bay. Several ships were lost, the long voyage had consumed the provisions, and several hundred men had been buried at sea. Then Admiral d'Enville died of apoplexy. Vice Admiral d'Estourmel succeeded to the command and called a council of officers. He proposed to attack Annapolis Royal rather than the more strongly fortified Louisbourg. When the decision went against him, he committed suicide! The third in command, the Marquis de la Jonquière, began collecting provisions from the Acadians. Camp was established ashore, but the epidemic could not be halted. As October advanced, the total number of dead reached nearly twenty-four hundred. Clothing from them was innocently given to some

French allied Indians, who were thereupon decimated by the same plague.

The English at Louisbourg knew of the sickness and waited. The Forty-sixth Regiment had been sent out for garrison duty. Reinforcements reached them from Governor Shirley, which number was inflated for the benefit of the French. La Jonquière persevered. He re-embarked his sick men, turning sixteen ships into floating hospitals, and headed for Annapolis Royal. Another storm dispersed the fleet. On October 27 La Jonquière held a council, and the officers not surprisingly voted to return to France. The fleet staggered through more storms, daily burying men at sea. Without ever firing at the enemy France suffered a grievous defeat.

Louis XV was undismayed. He outfitted another fleet for Admiral La Jonquière and sent him off to Louisbourg in May, 1747. Four days out he met a British fleet under Admirals Warren and Anson. That was the end. Six French ships were captured, including the admiral's flagship. Warren was knighted and elected to Parliament.

While this false alarm to the northward upset Shirley's plans for an aggressive move against Canada, it seemed to inspire stronger French raiding parties in 1747. Holding on to Beaubassin on the isthmus of Nova Scotia, Jean Roch de Ramezay learned that Colonel Arthur Noble with some Massachusetts troops was occupying Grand Pré on the other fork of the Bay of Fundy. Because they had arrived too late in the fall to build a fort, the English were quartered in a string of houses. Ramezay sent Coulon de Villiers (the man who was to force Washington's surrender at Fort Necessity in 1754) to lead a mixed force on a dreadful winter's march late in January, 1747, against Grand Pré. Picking up Acadians and priest-led Indians along the way, De Villiers swelled his force to five hundred, only to learn that it barely equaled the size of the enemy.

The attackers pressed on in swirling snow and formed themselves into a dozen parties to strike simultaneously at as many houses pointed out to them through the storm by local Acadian guides. Colonel Noble and some of his officers were killed in their beds. More than three hundred of the roused soldiers barricaded themselves in a great stone building and, after resisting all next day, surrendered with the honors of war. Minus eighty killed and about as many wounded, the Massachusetts men marched back to Annapolis Royal under oath not to fight again unless exchanged. The French, who had suffered about forty casualties, withdrew northward. In April Shirley sent troops to reoccupy Grand Pré.

Farther west Ensign Boucher de Niverville set out the first of April for the Connecticut River with a force which he boasted numbered seven hundred. If it did, he was not the man to lead them. They approached Number 4 again, which was now occupied by Captain Phineas Stevens and thirty men. The attack went on all day, but the French would not make what could only be a victorious assault. At night the ensign sent in a flag of truce and asked for a parley next morning. At the meeting Niverville demanded surrender or he would overrun the fort without mercy. Captain Stevens allowed as how he would talk it over with the boys. In town-meeting style they unanimously voted no. Stevens reported the result. Firing resumed and continued all that day, but no assault. On the third morning Niverville sent in another flag: would Monsieur Stevens care to sell him some provisions, if the besiegers would leave? Stevens made a counter offer: he would give them five bushels of corn in exchange for every English prisoner they had with them or back in Canada. The answer to this was another fusil-lade of shots, after which the French silently departed.

Commodore Charles Knowles of the British navy, then in Boston, sent Stevens a sword when he heard of his brave defense. As a result the later settlement at Number 4 was called Charlestown.

The Iroquois finally took to the warpath this same month of April. Captain Walter Butler led a company of Mohawks toward Crown Point and attacked a French party, killing eight. Chief Hendrick, a scar-faced warrior who had visited Queen Anne in 1710, led a mixed detachment of forty up to the St. Lawrence, where in June he was surprised on an island above Montreal and lost thirteen before escaping. Johnson reported to the governor that thirty-one prisoners were brought in by the Indians that spring.

More than three thousand troops were assembled around Albany for possible advance on Crown Point and even Montreal. Early in May, 1747, some of the Pennsylvania and New York units mutinied over lack of pay, especially after the New Jersey troops were paid in full. Governor Clinton daily expected money from England (these troops had been raised a year ago at Newcastle's behest). When he received the money in July he paid the troops and dismissed them. The Iroquois now complained with some justice that they had been decoyed into war with the French which the English now refused to prosecute.

On June 30 the French had attacked the Saratoga fort again. Thinking it merely a scouting force, the commandant ordered Lieutenant Joseph Chew and a hundred men to go out and dislodge them. Chew discovered that the force under Lieutenant Herbin amounted to five or six hundred Indians and French.

He lost fifteen killed and forty-nine captured. Colonel Peter Schuyler, namesake and nephew of Albany's late mayor, relieved the fort, but it was shortly abandoned and burned.

A reliable gauge of the extent of border warfare was the size of prisoner exchanges that were soon set in operation. A ship from Canada arrived in Boston on August 20, 1747, with two hundred and seventy-one captives released. They reported that seventy others had died and one hundred and thirty remained in Canada. Six weeks later a Massachusetts agent delivered sixty-three French prisoners to Île de Basque, below Quebec, and received sixteen more English captives.

Prosecution of the war from New England suffered a sudden, bitter turn from a Boston incident. Commodore Knowles, who had been admiring of colonial frontier defense, so far forgot his surroundings as to apply an accepted British naval practice. Needing additional crewmen for his five ships, he sent a press gang into town on November 17, 1747, to seize likely men for his squadron. To his astonishment, the reaction was immediate and violent. Part of the populace rose in noisy wrath and seized several of his officers. Governor Shirley issued a proclamation on November 21 against the "lewd and profligate persons, who being armed with cutlasses and other weapons" threatened naval officers, the sheriff, and the General Court. A town meeting was held that condemned the rioters and called for release of the officers held by the mob. Knowles then released the impressed Boston citizens and sailed away. The Royal Navy had been defeated in a manner that was symptomatic, had anyone paused to analyze the reaction. Old Salt Knowles was given a lesson in the sanctity of free persons in America, which London failed to remember.

Spain took little part in the war that resulted from her original conflict with England. Her privateers cruised off the Carolina and Georgia coast. American preoccupation with the French seemingly offered an opportunity for Florida to deliver blows against the southern coast, but perhaps the Floridanos hesitated because the Americans were mobilized. Not until August, 1747, did they carry out a raid. It was a small enterprise, directed against Beaufort, North Carolina. The town was plundered, but nothing of value was gained by the raid. As for Gibraltar and Minorca, no attempt was made against those British outposts.

The exchange of prisoners did not presume an end to the war. Late in May, 1748, Captain Eleazer Melvin took eighteen men out of Fort Dummer on a scout toward Lake Champlain. Reaching the shore they fired on a canoe containing a dozen Indians. How many were hit is not known, but an alarm was sounded at nearby Crown Point. Melvin now had to retreat as rapidly as he could to outrun pursuit. After a few days he felt himself safe enough to encamp on West River in southeastern Vermont. But his trackers had not given up and they caught up with him. Melvin lost six men in the confusion before he withdrew farther. He had fought under Captain Lovewell in 1725 and now suffered a similar defeat.

Two weeks later a party of thirteen men headed for Fort Dummer was attacked, with three killed and seven taken prisoner. Seizing the initiative again, Captain Humphrey Hobbs led forty men out of Number 4 on a scout. He soon found himself stalked by one hundred and fifty Indians. The encounter developed into a four-hour running fight in which Hobbs lost four killed and three wounded, but the Indians broke off after their chief was shot.

Early July brought welcome news of preliminary articles

of peace between France and England, but no suggestion of relaxing hostilities. The Indians who attacked Captain Hobbs hovered around Fort Dummer and waylaid an approaching party of seventeen men under Sergeant Thomas Taylor. Six were killed and eight made prisoner. Then the Indians burned some cabins near Schenectady and killed twelve Dutch inhabitants. The alarm sent seventy men under Lieutenant John Darling in pursuit. The Yorkers found the marauders, and both sides eagerly engaged in battle. The Indians were driven off, but not until nine of the troops had been killed, including the lieutenant, and four captured.

July was also the month of a third Iroquois congress at Albany. About fourteen hundred and fifty Indians attended and were addressed by agents of several colonies. Presents were distributed generously to keep the tribes favorably disposed toward the English and deaf to the blandishments of the French. Governor Clinton told them to listen only to William Johnson's words. The Iroquois declared a readiness to join any English expedition northward, although they still were disappointed over the failure to invade Canada a year ago.

Another ship from Quebec arrived in Boston in August with one hundred and seventy-five more captives. They reported that a similar number had died as prisoners. From Louisbourg came another vessel with a "great number" of captives. Eighty-two prisoners were brought to Charleston from Cape François, San Domingo. The war was running out. In a final thrust the Spaniards struck at the southern coast again. A task force landed September 3 and captured Brunswick, North Carolina, on Cape Fear River. While the Spaniards were plundering the town, the ejected inhabitants returned in force and drove them out. One of the Spanish ships blew up and sank.

The Treaty of Aix-la-Chapelle was signed on October 18,

1748, and news of it reached Boston just before Christmas. The treaty was not published there until March, 1749. Much as peace was welcome, the terms did not excite jubilation in New England. Britain considered her side victorious, and France initiated the negotiations. Nevertheless, Louis XV insisted upon the restoration of Cape Breton Island (to defend the St. Lawrence) as his price for peace. George II finally agreed, partly because Madras in India was being returned to England and partly because mere territory to enlarge the empire formed no part of ministerial thinking at this time. A joint commission was to be appointed to determine the boundary of Nova Scotia and other matters. Maria Theresa was recognized as ruler of Austria, but Prussia kept Silesia. French troops withdrew from Dutch cities. Spain achieved none of her territorial ambitions and agreed to revive the Asiento contract for four years. The right of search, over which England and Spain had gone to war, was not mentioned. Nothing was changed in America. The treaty signalized Prussia's rise to power in Europe, even as it marked Holland's decline. What had b⟨...⟩ but still was not clear to England, wa⟨...⟩ fight France on the Continent.

This short war had cost several times more fatalities from disease and captivity than from military action. Even so, those who died from weapons exceeded those killed in Queen Anne's War. Rough estimates show at least five hundred Americans killed and more than eleven hundred dead of disease or exposure, not counting the heavy toll from the Cartagena expedition in 1741. On the French side, perhaps only three hundred and fifty were killed, but the disastrous naval expedition probably accounted for more than twenty-five hundred deaths from disease.

The capture of Louisbourg has been called the most important military achievement of the American colonies before the Revolution, and the only British success of any importance during the War of the Austrian Succession. It was not the most important battle of the colonial wars, but it did involve the largest number of Americans and was a siege undertaken and directed by them, without the help of British army officers. It had several distinctively American touches about it. Planned by a lawyer, executed by a merchant commanding undisciplined farmers, fishermen, and mechanics, it was successful because of initial luck (which the Yankees quickly forgot), followed up by enthusiastic action. There was a festival air about the whole proceeding that inspired a contemporary comparison to "a Cambridge Commencement." The results were both pleasant and dangerous. The victors developed supreme self-confidence and a corresponding contempt for, or at least indifference to, professional armies and military engineers. Louisbourg, therefore, emerged from the war as a symbol of American prowess, as if a new military power had appeared in the New World.

As for the second declaration above, it is true that British arms did not distinguish themselves in the European theater. Dettingen was an escape from a trap rather than a victory. Culloden was a one-sided clash not fought against the regular enemy. The French defeated the English twice: at Fontenoy and at Laffeldt. It was two British naval victories in 1747, by Anson and Warren off Cape Finisterre and by Hawk off Belleisle, that brought about treaty negotiations.

Consequently, the rashest measure Great Britain could take was to hand Louisbourg back to the French as if it were a bauble or a remote barren island—especially after the British admiralty in the glow of victory in 1745 had threatened to hang any man who would dare to surrender it. American pride was insulted, and New England turned bitter. Americans would not respond so enthusiastically in the next war with France. As they clearly foresaw, in another war Louisbourg would have to be taken again, and the lobster-backs could jolly well do the job themselves. When the necessity did arise, it required nine thousand British regulars and forty ships of war.

VI

attempt to mend ways and call a draw

French Militia vs. Virginia Militia

The Treaty of Aix-la-Chapelle resembled the Treaty of Ryswick in being a truce that provided for mutual restoration of conquests and prisoners and permitted the strengthening of defenses. Truces are always temporary, and this one lasted a year longer than the 1697 armistice. France and England had taken each other's measure and declared a draw: the French army could beat the British army, the British navy could whip the French navy. As for what the Canadians and New Englanders could do, that was not for keeps anyway.

One step was taken toward solution of the troublesome old problem of the boundaries of Acadia, or Nova Scotia. A joint commission was appointed to determine the just and true bounds. At the same time a new town, named Halifax, was founded in 1749 on the southeast coast by twenty-five hundred emigrants shipped directly from England. It became the capital, grew rapidly with settlers from New England, and the Forty-seventh Regiment was posted there as protection. The boundary dispute was perhaps more symptomatic of latent conflicts than it was a separate problem capable of independent solution. The commission finally met in 1750. On the British side it consisted of Governor Shirley of Massachusetts and William Mildmay of London; for the French were Governor Galissonière of Canada, a hunchbacked man of science, and M. de Silhouette of Paris. Two of the men thus were familiar with American geography, but that was not enough to steer the commission toward agreement. Britain presented a historical argument for broad bounds which the French could not demolish, so they turned to their other business of determining ownership of certain small West Indies islands. When that discussion reached an impasse because France would not first evacuate them as she originally agreed to do, the commission swerved to its third charge, the matter of prizes taken during the war. Clearly there was procrastination on the French side, while the two Englishmen unhappily quarreled. Shirley was recalled in April, 1752, and replaced, although he was returned to Massachusetts for a second term as governor. The British ministry realized that the joint commission was getting nowhere, yet it did not want to be the one to terminate this diplomatic effort.

What most roiled the troubled waters was French advances into the Ohio Valley—at the very moment Virginia speculators were eyeing the same region. There seemed to be simultaneous realization that here was the true prize, the high stake of contest, rather than the precise measurements of Nova Scotia, the guarantees of fishing rights, or a West India island or two. Empire lay west, in the American continent's vast rich interior.

The Colonial Wars

The French were determined to join Canada and Louisiana, not merely by the cord of the Mississippi River, but also by a broad belt of forts and missions spotted across the Ohio Valley. The English were equally intent on expanding inland beyond the Appalachians and prohibiting France from erecting a fence down the west side of the seaboard colonies.

Both powers felt they had historic rights to the area. Quite aside from the fact that some of the English colonial charters ran magnanimously from sea to sea, the Iroquois had been recognized by France since 1713 as British subjects, and the Iroquois claimed the Ohio Valley by right of conquest. Britain had obtained transfer of title from the Iroquois by purchase in the Treaty of Lancaster, 1744. The French claimed the valley by arguing that La Salle had reached the Ohio River in 1679 and asserted his country's dominion over it. This premise was actually a surmise from La Salle's ambiguous journal, and modern scholarship has concluded that La Salle never saw the Ohio. What gave ground for dispute was that neither nation had any settlements in the valley, and possession, then as now, was the most potent evidence of ownership.

Virginia, whose charter expanded its boundaries westward in a widening V, had made several grants of land to individuals before and during the war, with the approval of the Board of Trade and the Privy Council. When several land promoters and speculators formed the Ohio Company of Virginia early in 1749 and applied to the colonial council, they obtained two hundred thousand acres of land on the south side of the Ohio River, with the promise of three hundred thousand acres more as soon as settlement of a hundred families was achieved. At the same time, the Loyal Land Company obtained a grant of eight hundred thousand acres to the west. Other smaller grants were made. The Blue Ridge no longer loomed as a wall.

The French reply was a Gallic gesture. Unable to promote settlements, the Canadian governor, the Comte de la Galis-sonière, dispatched Captain Pierre Joseph Céloron de Blain-ville on a circular tour of claim staking. Céloron knew the lakes; he had commanded at Detroit and Niagara before the war, and at Crown Point in 1747. He was now fifty-six and headed a curious expedition of eight officers, six cadets, a chaplain (Father Bonnecamp), two hundred soldiers, and about thirty Indians. The party left Monteal on June 15, 1749, and moved up river. At the mouth of the Oswegatchie River (Ogdensburg, New York) it found a Sulpician priest building a mission post to counteract the English Fort Oswego. On July 6 the band reached Fort Niagara and began the week's portage around the falls.

From the east end of Lake Erie, Céloron carried to Lake Chautauqua and on July 29 entered the head of the Allegheny River, then considered the beginning of the Ohio. At modern Warren, Pennsylvania he tacked up a metal sign decorated with the king's arms and buried his first lead plate of claim. It gave notice "of the renewal of possession which we have taken of the said river Ohio, and of all those which fall into it, and of all the territories on both sides as far as the source of the said rivers, as the preceding kings of France have enjoyed or ought to have enjoyed it and which they have maintained by arms and by treaties, particularly by those of Ryswick, Utrecht, and Aix-la-Chapelle."

Even this brief declaration of prior ownership contained some bombast, because none of the treaties mentioned contain any reference to the Ohio Valley—as, in fact, France was to argue a few years hence. By implication they simply reinstated the conflicting claims.

About nine miles downstream Céloron came upon a village of Senecas and held a council. The chiefs were told that the English were invading French lands; if any were in this village they should be expelled. The Senecas promised compliance, but Céloron was sophisticated enough not to believe them. At the town of Venango (Franklin, Pennsylvania), the Indians fled with two English traders into the woods, one of whom was John Fraser, long established there. Céloron buried another lead plate. The same emptiness greeted him at the Delaware village of Attique (Kittaning, Pennsylvania). At Chartier's Town the French found only six English traders. Céloron ordered them out and sent by them a letter to the governor of Pennsylvania expressing surprise at their trespass on French territory.

The expedition passed the empty site of modern Pittsburgh. At modern McKee's Rocks, the village of Queen Allaquippa was empty, but six more English traders were warned off. Beyond was Chiningué, or Logstown (near modern Economy, Pennsylvania), a large village of Mingos, Delawares, and Shawnees, and a big trading center with several Englishmen in attendance. The inhabitants appeared hostile to the visitors. Nevertheless, Céloron stayed three days and held councils. He delivered his governor's message, which accused the English of intending to "rob you of your country . . . which belongs to me." If the Indians believed the first part, they hardly conceded the last. Here Céloron reported the basic obstacle to his mission: the English were able to sell the Indians goods for about one-fourth the French price. Warning the traders to leave, he continued his river journey.

At the entrance of Wheeling Creek another plate went into the ground; at the mouth of the Muskingum another; and at the Great Kanawha still another—silent, hidden, ineffective claims to a vast wilderness. At the Scioto River a large Shawnee town threatened the French but finally agreed to a council. Céloron repeated his messages, this time omitting the claim of the French king to the land. The English traders were too numerous to seize, so they were warned and the cavalcade passed on. Father Bonnecamp observed that the Ohio was "little known to the French and, unfortunately, too well known to the English."

On August 30 at the mouth of the Great Miami the last lead plate was entombed, and Céloron turned northward. Far up its shallow course he reached a Miami village called Pickawillany (Piqua, Ohio), ruled by a chief named La Demoiselle but nicknamed Old Britain because of his hospitality to English traders. Céloron tried to persuade him to move his people back to the main Miami settlement at the head of the Maumee River (Fort Wayne, Indiana), where he would be less accessible to the English, but the chief demurred. Indeed, the village prospered and rapidly increased its population later. Here the French abandoned their canoes and tramped overland to Fort Miamis (Fort Wayne), where there was a small and sickly French garrison. New canoes permitted them to move down the river to Lake Erie and up to Detroit. They then returned across the lakes to Fort Frontenac and Montreal, the arduous journey having disclosed how fruitfully the English had penetrated the Ohio Valley, which the French hoped to exploit.

The Colonial Wars

Céloron found that Governor Galissonière had been succeeded by the luckless admiral, the Marquis de la Jonquière, with the admonition that the French must establish themselves in some fashion on the Ohio River. The new governor licensed several traders to set up business at Logstown, which became an active French center of influence in the next two years.

Now the Ohio Company of Virginia bestirred itself. It had built a storehouse in 1749 on the Virginia side of the Potomac opposite the mouth of Wills Creek (Cumberland, Maryland). The first cargo of goods for the western trade arrived in March, 1750; Indians and traders snapped them up. Late in the year the company engaged Christopher Gist to explore the region granted to it and submit a detailed description. He found Pennsylvania traders well represented along the Ohio. In early 1751 he pushed on to Pickawillany, where he was joyfully received. Closer to home, on the borders of Pennsylvania, he had found the Delawares and Mingos (who were emigrant Senecas) more suspicious of the English because of French tales. Further, the Pennsylvania traders out of self-interest had corroborated the French accusations that the Virginians in particular were after the Indian lands. George Croghan was chief Indian agent for the governor of Pennsylvania and he persuaded the Delawares that they would benefit most from an English —that is, Pennsylvanian—fort and trading house at modern Pittsburgh. But when the governor sought funds, the Assembly rejected the whole idea. It remained for Virginia to oppose the French. First, so as to confirm the Treaty of Lancaster and buy the western land again from its inhabitants, Virginia called the Iroquois to a council at Logstown in June, 1752, with the Delawares, Shawnees, and Hurons who lived along the Ohio. The Indians acquiesced.

French vs. Virginia Militia

Governor Jonquière died and was succeeded in 1752 by the Marquis Duquesne. Arrogant and stubborn, Duquesne determined to extend French rule, not just commerce, into the Ohio country. In the West two menacing steps had already been taken more or less upon local authority. The French built a fort on Sandusky Bay, where some disgruntled Hurons had a village open to Pennsylvania traders. Then to chastise the Anglophile Miamis at Pickawillany, a mixed force of Canadians and Indians under half-breed Charles Michel de Langlade of Michilimackinac descended on the town in June, 1752, and burned it, killed Old Britain, and seized five English traders. The disillusioned Miamis trekked back to their nation's headquarters at the head of the Maumee.

Working closely with the intendant, François Bigot, Governor Duquesne laid plans during the fall of 1752 for establishing a fort on the Ohio River. Captain Claude Pécaudy de Contrecœur, commandant of Fort Niagara, was secretly ordered to improve the portage road around the falls for the passage of two thousand men and their supplies early in the spring. Three forts were to be constructed on the way to the Ohio River. Command of the expedition was entrusted to the veteran Sieur de Marin, who had lined his pockets in partnership with Bigot while commanding the fur post at modern Green Bay, Wisconsin. Second in command was Captain Michel Péan, Contrecœur's nephew and not yet thirty but sufficiently ambitious to let his wife become Bigot's mistress. The purchase of supplies allowed splendid opportunity for Bigot and himself to peculate. The engineer who would design and build the forts was Captain François Le Mercier, who also accumulated considerable wealth during his service. How honest the governor was in the midst of this corruption is not known, but the weakening of Canada financially under Bigot's grasping and devious hand for thirteen years was well launched and was not to be discovered for another nine years.

Upon information from a voyageur, Duquesne decided on a new route south of Niagara and ordered the first fort to be constructed at Presque Île (Erie, Pennsylvania). An advance work party reached the site in May, 1753. Captains Marin and Le Mercier arrived in June and finished the fort. The second outpost, located at the head of Rivière aux Bœufs (French Creek), was started in July and called Fort Le Bœuf (Waterford, Pennsylvania). A square of pickets, it was somewhat smaller than Fort Presque Île. A road to it also was cut and new boats were built. Captain Péan brought the rear guard to Niagara and moved forward to join his chief in September. On August 28 Joncaire de Chabert seized the trading post at Venango which had been occupied for several years by John Fraser. The trading post was at the mouth of French Creek (Franklin, Pennsylvania), where it flowed into the Ohio (i.e., Allegheny) River.

Now the Mingos grew apprehensive about this solid invasion of their country. A Seneca chief, Tanachrison, protested to Captain Marin in September and even warned him not to descend the Allegheny. Marin replied that the Ohio River belonged to the French king, who was interested only in "protecting" the nations that lived along its banks and helping supply their necessities. Marin was gambling on the chief's having no great following and he was correct.

The New York Iroquois, who claimed the region, remained neutral despite the efforts of William Johnson to stir up hostility. At a general conference of the Six Nations, September 8–10, Johnson told the chiefs that the French and their Indians were moving toward the Ohio with intention of establishing themselves there. "Is it with your consent or leave that they proceed in this extraordinary manner?" he asked.

The Iroquois denied giving any such permission. "We don't know what you Christians, English and French together, intend; we are so hemmed in by both that we have hardly a hunting place left." Obviously they were not going to threaten the French. The province of New York was in process of changing royal governors and was more worried about the French at Crown Point. It hoped that Pennsylvania or Virginia would act to offset the enemy thrust by erecting western posts of their own.

French advance was brought to a halt in 1753, though not by Indian or English threat. Fever, scurvy, and exhaustion began taking their toll from the soldier-workmen, and drought set back the time schedule for descent of the river. Of the more than two thousand men on duty at the beginning of summer, only eight hundred were fit for service in the fall. To push farther south in the face of coming winter seemed too dangerous and difficult. Marin sent Péan and Le Mercier back to Montreal with most of the troops. He remained at Fort Le Bœuf, where on October 29, 1753, he died.

English reaction began to bubble, with Lieutenant Governor Robert Dinwiddie of Virginia stirring the brew. Sixty years old and ambitious for his province, he was more than willing to take the lead in stemming the French invasion. He had sought permission from London in June to build some forts on the Ohio for defense, without mentioning how useful they would be to the aims of the Ohio Company, of which he was also a member. The reply from the Earl of Holderness, secretary of state, was dated August 28 and gave him royal approval,

build on Ohio River *delivered message*

at the expense of the colony, and said that cannon were being sent. Dinwiddie should, however, first represent to any intruders "our undoubted rights to such parts of the said river Ohio, as are within the limits of our province of Virginia, or any other [of] our province or provinces in America." Then if trespassers, European or Indian, should fail to leave or obstruct these orders, "our will and pleasure is, that you should repell force by force."

Dinwiddie received these instructions in October and, nothing loath to act, dispatched on the thirtieth a twenty-one-year-old militia officer named George Washington, "a person of distinction" (he was already a major), to carry a warning message to the French commandant on French Creek. He was accompanied by Christopher Gist as guide, two interpreters, and three others. The party went by way of Wills Creek and passed John Fraser's new trading post on the Monongahela (Braddock, Pennsylvania), then the forks of the Ohio (which Washington noted as an ideal site for a fort), and down river to Logstown where an Indian bodyguard might be obtained. But only four Indians would go: the disgruntled Tanachrison; a young warrior named Kyashuta, who in ten years would help stir Indian revolt against the British; and two others.

The party reached Fraser's captured post at Venango, from which a French flag was flying, on December 4, 1753. Captain Joncaire, brother of the more notorious Indian agent Joncaire de Chabert, greeted them hospitably. He promised Major Washington that his message should be delivered to the commandant at Fort Le Bœuf. Tanachrison tried to return the French wampum he had received in September, to emphasize that he rejected the French claim to the Ohio, but Joncaire got him drunk and refused the belt.

French vs. Virginia Militia

Rain and snow delayed Washington, and he did not get to Fort Le Bœuf until December 11. The new commandant, Captain Jacques Legardeur de St. Pierre, politely received Governor Dinwiddie's letter "requiring" him to decamp.

Captain St. Pierre penned a reply, saying that he wished Dinwiddie's letter could have been sent to the governor of Canada, as he would have set forth the evidence of France's rights to the lands along the Ohio; but the message would be forwarded and in the meantime St. Pierre did not think himself obliged to obey the summons. The letter was polished, courteous, and firm.

The French officers were less suave toward Washington's Indians, offering every argument and gift to win them to their side. The Indians all departed with Washington, but they stopped at Venango for Captain Joncaire's liquor and presents. Washington set out on December 23 and had a rugged journey back to Williamsburg, which he reached on January 16, 1754. The governor was so impressed by the acute observations in Washington's Journal that he ordered it to be printed. It gave quite an impression of French machinations against the English colonies.

Dinwiddie got permission of his council to call out two hundred militia to protect the workmen who were ready to erect a fort at modern Pittsburgh for the Ohio Company. He wrote to seven other governors to help in "the common cause," and called the House of Burgesses to meet on February 14, when they voted £10,000 to support additional troops and assert Virginia's right to the Ohio lands. Still, the whole dispute seemed rather remote to some of the burgesses, primarily a contest between rival land companies. Royal concern was certainly vague: foreign intruders must be expelled from English do-

131

minions, without specifying what the western boundary of those dominions was. Governor James Hamilton of Pennsylvania, whose Quaker Assembly would not let him do anything, was not too disappointed: "I presume this letter [from Holderness] was wrote merely in order to get rid of some importunity on the part of the government of Virginia, or of the Ohio Company: otherwise, when it orders us to repel force by force, but restricts us to the undoubted limits of His Majesty's dominions, it would certainly have pointed out to us what these limits were, which by all enquiry I have been able to make, I could never find had been settled or ascertained. Besides that, it looks like knowing very little of America to expect that Maryland and New Jersey will concern themselves about what is doing at Ohio. . . ."

Not until April 2, 1754, were the first two companies of Virginia militia ready to march, and they totaled one hundred and twenty rather than two hundred. Commanded by Major Washington, they were to protect the fort-builders, who had now been on the site two months. The contingent proceeded slowly by way of Wills Creek.

Spring had also put the French in motion once more. The new commander, Captain Contrecœur, led more than a thousand men from French Creek down the Allegheny toward the forks. The Virginia work party of forty-one was surprised on April 17, and Ensign Edward Ward had no choice but to surrender. He was allowed to march his men back to Wills Creek, meeting Washington on the way.

The French force now in possession of the forks of the Ohio demolished the fort that the Virginians had begun and started a much larger one, which they called Fort Duquesne. Washington sent the bitter news back to Governor Dinwiddie but clung to his original objective of recovering the site and driving the French away. He determined to push on as far as the Ohio Company's new storehouse on the Monongahela River at Red-stone Creek (two miles north of modern Brownsville) and there await large reinforcements. The forward movement was necessary, he felt, in order to retain the help of the anti-French Indians. But widening a trail into a wagon road was tediously slow work, and Washington's force could not make four miles a day.

His route followed or paralleled today's U.S. 40 westward and northwestward toward modern Uniontown, Pennsylvania. By May 24 he had reached the Great Meadows, between Laurel Hill and Chestnut Ridge. Christopher Gist brought him word that an advance party of French was lurking ahead. Seizing the opportunity, Washington marched northward at night with forty men, and early on May 28 surprised the French at a spot about five miles east of modern Uniontown. Ten of them, in-cluding their leader, Ensign Joseph Coulon de Jumonville, were killed, and all but one of the twenty-three survivors were cap-tured and sent back to Virginia.

As soon as word reached Fort Duquesne, Captain Con-trecœur prepared a larger detachment of five hundred French and a dozen Indians before he heard that Governor Duquesne was sending more Indians under the Sieur Coulon de Villiers, Jumonville's brother.

Washington, who had returned to the Great Meadows, began to fortify his camp, calling the rude stockade Fort Necessity. It is about ten miles southeast of Uniontown. There he was notified of his promotion to colonel and was joined by three new companies of Virginia militia, and an Independent Company of regulars from South Carolina who refused to work on road-building and would not take orders from a colonial colonel. The reinforcements, bringing the total number of men to nearly four hundred and fifty, immediately created a crisis in supplies, as the flour contractor had failed to deliver.

Washington moved his militia forward to continue the road-making, still hampered by lack of horses and flour. On June 28 he had news that the French and Indians were approaching and regretfully he called in his units to Fort Necessity. A few bags of flour arrived, and two more Independent Companies from New York were on their way. The fort was enlarged and somewhat strengthened by the hungry men, but the Indian allies melted away, fearful of the French after observing the crude fort. On July 3 it rained for hours, and the French came in view.

The enemy methodically killed all the cows and horses first and then began firing on the troops who lay in watery trenches. The musket fire lasted all afternoon, until a cloudburst put an end to it. In the dark the French called for a parley. Captain de Villiers said that since their two kings were at peace, he demanded only that the English return to Virginia and release the Frenchmen taken with Jumonville, for whose return two English officers must remain as hostages. Colonel Washington surveyed his camp: he had thirteen killed, fifty-four wounded, and almost a hundred sick; he had three days' provisions, no transport, and wet powder. Having been accorded the "honors of war," he signed the capitulation at midnight.

Among the water-stained articles, written in French which Washington could not read, was a clause by which he admitted having "assassinated" Jumonville, who was said to have been carrying a message to him, an absurd interpretation of an act of war but one having great propaganda value for the French.

Having suffered two rebuffs, Virginia gave up its independent effort to oust the French and asked for help from London. Virginia's lone effort had collapsed. While waiting, Governor Dinwiddie thought it better to break down the regiment of Virginia militia into separate companies, like the regulars. Such action deprived Washington of his colonelcy and reduced him to a captaincy. In annoyance and disappointment he resigned his commission and set about leasing Mount Vernon from his half-brother's widow. He was going to become a planter.

The Virginia Assembly provided more generously for defense in 1755, and before the year was out Dinwiddie learned that England was sending two regiments of regulars to spearhead the militia from several colonies in an irresistible advance against the French invaders at the Ohio forks.

It should be remembered that in spite of these warlike actions on the frontier, England and France were at peace and their joint commission was still arguing over the matters left to its determination in 1748. Yet France's minister had authorized Governor Duquesne to assert her right to the Ohio Valley by building forts on the river route, while the English cabinet had advised Governor Dinwiddie to do the same and "repell force by force." In brief, both countries had issued blank checks for acts of war, although England hoped to delay war in Europe until Spain declared herself neutral and until an ally was found to safeguard Hanover.

A clash in America was inevitable, and with concession or retreat out of local hands, Paris and London were going to be swept into war unless one side backed down completely. Meek surrender was out of the question when the stake was as rich as the Ohio Valley. The eve of the last and greatest of the colonial wars for supremacy in North America was darkening.

While Virginia was making these warlike advances and retreats, her governor was prevented from attending a congress of representatives from seven other colonies at Albany, New York, in June, 1754. Twenty-three distinguished men from Massachusetts, New Hampshire, Connecticut, Rhode Island, Pennsylvania, and Maryland gathered upon invitation of Lieutenant Governor James Delancey of New York to concert their efforts to renew friendship with the Iroquois and to explore united defense measures. Chief Hendrick, a steadfast friend of William Johnson, listed the complaints of the Iroquois: Englishmen had taken Mohawk land and furnished too much rum to the Indians while neglecting more useful gifts; Virginia and Pennsylvania were encroaching on Iroquois-claimed land in the West as much as Canada was; and Albany traders were selling arms to the French while the Iroquois were being urged to attack them. Though all these complaints were true, Delancey felt obliged to deny them. During the councils Pennsylvania bought a tract on the west side of the Susquehanna, and so did Connecticut secretly, thus laying a foundation for future dispute over the Wyoming Valley. By July 9 the Iroquois were brought around to expressions of good will, and they departed with thirty wagons loaded with gifts.

Other and potentially more important business also had claimed the attention of the union-minded delegates. They adopted in principle a proposal put forward by Benjamin Franklin of Philadelphia that the colonies form a union for defense, to be imposed by an act of Parliament. Details of such a confederation were then worked out calling for a President

French vs. Virginia Militia

General appointed by the Crown and a Grand Council elected by the colonies. Also recommended were certain immediate defense measures: repulse of the French invasion, a single superintendent for Indian affairs, a fort in each Indian nation, war vessels on the lakes, and a western boundary of the Appalachians for the existing colonies below New York so that new colonies could be established westward. The Albany plan so adopted was submitted to each of the seven colonial assemblies—and was not ratified by any one of them! It envisaged too much too soon. Since they failed to act, nothing occurred in England concerning the plan. Whether she would have fallen in with the Albany plan is not known. The coming war would reveal a dangerous lack of unified defense or offense which confederation would have overcome.

Meanwhile, anxiety in the British ministry led to consultation with the Duke of Cumberland, the son of George II, respected for his military knowledge as well as his rank. Government was ready to try the plan of 1711, 1740, and 1746 of recruiting Americans into regular regiments at British expense and under a British commander, since the colonial assemblies were so indifferent about paying for their own defense. Cumberland favored dispatching two Irish regiments (the Forty-fourth and Forty-eighth), to be raised to full strength in America, and a British commander in chief who would exercise authority over them plus the three regiments in Nova Scotia (the Fortieth, Forty-sixth, and Forty-seventh), the seven Independent Companies in New York and South Carolina, the two regiments promised Shirley and Pepperrell (the Fiftieth and Fifty-first) to be raised in America, and the militia of Virginia and Maryland. The colonies were to provide provisions, recruits, and quarters, collect wagons and horses, and contribute to a common defense fund at the disposal of the commander in chief. This plan for a combined force was adopted, its objective limited to ousting the French from what was considered English territory. Such a formidable army was sure to succeed, London thought.

VII

British Regulars and American Militia

Early in 1755 there arrived in Virginia Lieutenant Colonel Sir John St. Clair to serve as deputy quartermaster general to the regular and provincial forces. He at once went to work stockpiling supplies at the Wills Creek stronghold, now styled Fort Cumberland. Reviewing the three Independent Companies there, he promptly discharged forty of the most decrepit men. His manner indicated resoluteness and dispatch, qualities conspicuously lacking in the colonial supply service. His contracts for horses, rations, powder, etc., were several times the outlay for the 1754 expedition.

Near the end of February the new commander in chief of the British forces in North America reached Williamsburg. He was Major General Edward Braddock, sixty years old, an officer experienced more in garrison than battlefield, and a tough disciplinarian. Blunt and haughty, he was temperamentally the opposite of Commodore Warren, for instance, but he had been selected for his assignment by the Duke of Cumberland, Britain's foremost soldier. Braddock arrived in advance of the two incomplete Irish regiments: the Forty-fourth under Sir Peter Halkett and the Forty-eighth under Colonel Thomas Dunbar.

Civilian George Washington met Braddock and was offered a position as aide-de-camp with a temporary commission as captain. The twenty-three-year-old proprietor of Mount Vernon accepted the position but not the commission; he who had once been a colonel preferred to serve as a volunteer, without pay. The operation of Mount Vernon was entrusted to a younger brother, and Washington joined Braddock at Alexandria in April.

The strategy for the coming campaign included three objectives. Braddock was to drive the French from Fort Duquesne and then perhaps assist in the taking of Fort Niagara, although the primary attack there would come from Governor William Shirley as major general. The third thrust was to be against Fort St. Frédéric at Crown Point by William Johnson, the New York Indian agent, at the head of the northern militia. There was further talk of a campaign in Nova Scotia by the three regiments there. In conference with Shirley and several governors on these measures, Braddock was infuriated to learn that the colonies were not going to provide him with a common defense fund—indeed, Pennsylvania would not offer any money for warfare—and he was loudly impatient with their slowness in finding recruits and wagons. Braddock's secretary, who was Governor Shirley's son, was acute enough to observe: "We have a general most judiciously chosen for being disqualified for the service he is employed in, in almost every respect."

British Regulars and American Militia

The two Irish regiments and Braddock were encamped at Wills Creek on May 10, 1755. They still were not filled out to strength. Frontier difficulties already familiar to Washington now delayed the expedition further. The regular officers of exalted reputation showed themselves to be unresourceful, inefficient, and even stupid. Their failures were compounded by the indifference, avarice, and laziness of the local civilians who were supposed to help equip the military. What little material was available cost excessively.

While Braddock was stomping impatiently around Fort Cumberland, Lieutenant Governor Charles Lawrence of Nova Scotia was with reason worried over his position. Although the boundaries of his province had not been determined officially, there was no question in English minds that at the very least the whole peninsula belonged to King George. The French boldly disputed even this; they had established two ambitious forts and several fortified posts along the north edge of the peninsula. The two main forts were Beauséjour, just off the Missaguash River at the head of Chignecto Bay, and Gaspereau on the west shore of Baye Verte. Almost a third of the Acadians, or five thousand, were openly pro-French; the rest were "neutral" but sympathetic to French dominion. Whereas the French could arm sixteen hundred Acadians, call up four hundred Abenakis and Micmacs under their fighting priest, Abbé Le Loutre, and summon several hundred regulars from Louisbourg, Governor Lawrence had less than sixteen hundred regulars in the three regiments there and about thirteen hundred doubtful militia from around Halifax.

In November, 1754, he had appealed to Governor Shirley to help him take the initiative and drive out the French before they overran the whole of Nova Scotia. Governor Duquesne

141

had already written to the Abbé Le Loutre and the commandant of Fort Beauséjour "to devise a plausible pretext for attacking" the English. Lieutenant Colonel Robert Monckton carried Lawrence's letter to Boston, where Shirley had already received orders from London to aid Lawrence in reclaiming Nova Scotia. That energetic executive, who was recruiting a regiment and planning two expeditions into New York province, won the secret approval of the General Court to raise two thousand militia, to be paid from England. Monckton was given the command. Delayed until the arrival of small arms and powder, the corps sailed northward late in May, 1755, and landed safely under cover of a fog at Fort Lawrence, southeast of Fort Beauséjour. Augmented by two hundred and fifty regulars, the expedition marched northward to get between Beauséjour and Gaspereau.

On June 6 the Acadians burned the village and church of Beauséjour and retired into the fort. Monckton brought up the cannon that had been pulled along by the foot soldiers. Captain Louis de Vergor had been taken almost by surprise. He rounded up more than a thousand militia to help his garrison. The cannonade that began on June 14 demoralized them and they demanded to leave. The Abbé Le Loutre escaped. Captain Vergor surrendered on the sixteenth with permission for his regulars to go to Louisbourg. The Acadians were pardoned because they said they had been forced to take up arms. Monckton turned on Fort Gaspereau and sent to the commandant a copy of the terms granted to Captain Vergor. When the New England troops appeared, the fort capitulated on the same terms. Louisbourg, now isolated from French Canada, would have to be supplied from the Atlantic.

After more than forty years of indulgence toward the recalcitrant Acadians, the British government finally determined upon harsh measures to solve the dilemma of this pocket of British citizens who refused all duties and responsibilities of allegiance to England while enjoying religious freedom and exemption from military obligations and even taxes, privileges they could never have enjoyed as French citizens. Misled by their church leaders, they adopted a stubborn hostile attitude that would not be reconciled to their legal status. When the government demanded that they take an unrestricted oath of allegiance, the inhabitants firmly refused. They were then considered alien enemies and in July, 1755, were ordered deported. To send them into Canada, or to France from whence they would presumably be transported to Canada, would have only strengthened the enemy. To send them to England would have burdened the country with an unassimilable bloc. The final alternative was to scatter them among the English colonies, which did not welcome them either. Many escaped to Canada, but more than six thousand were taken away. A similar number was deported later, after the capture of Cape Breton Island and Prince Edward Island. Almost all the latter went to France and were repaid with ill treatment for their fidelity. Many hundreds eventually returned to Nova Scotia, took the oath of allegiance to the English Crown, and resettled.

Braddock's expedition finally consisted of the two regiments of regulars, with sixty artillerists and thirty seamen, the three Independent Companies, and eleven companies of militia from Virginia, North Carolina, and Maryland—a total of twenty-five hundred men. Such was the road, however, the inferior horses, and the insufficient number of wagons that, after starting from Fort Cumberland on June 7, the column averaged only about two miles a day, an impossibly slow march, as it had a hundred and ten miles to go. In desperation Braddock asked young Washington what should be done. The Virginian advised pushing on swiftly with a detachment and some artillery, leaving most of the wagons to come along behind. Accordingly a column of thirteen hundred of the best men, under Colonel Halkett, was put in motion on June 20. Later one hundred and fifty additional men were sent forward with more supplies.

Progress was still slow, but the column crossed the Youghiogheny and reached the banks of the Monongahela, where it turned northward. Signs of Indians were detected, but no enemy was seen. At length the right bank of the river tilted so precipitately that the expedition decided to ford the Monongahela, march down the left bank for two miles, and recross just below the mouth of Turtle Creek, where John Fraser had his new trading house. Everyone expected an enemy attack to come during this maneuver, eight to ten miles from Fort Duquesne.

Early on the morning of July 9 Lieutenant Colonel Thomas Gage, who would later become commander in chief in America and touch off the American Revolution, led out the van and secured both crossings. By early afternoon the column was at the second crossing. There was reported to be open ground about an hour's march ahead, where the last camp would be made. Gage resumed his place at the head with four hundred and fifty troops and a few scouts as flankers, although the trail was bordered on either side by ravines with dense undergrowth. Farther to the right a hill dominated the area. Passing it, Gage did not send a platoon to occupy it, as he had done once earlier in a similar location. In this wild terrain Braddock

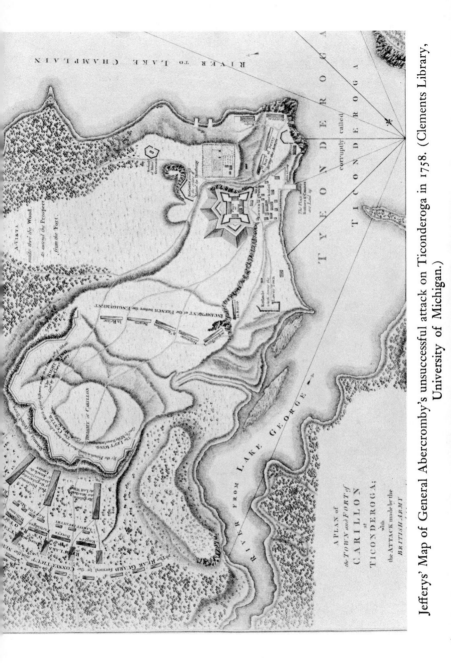

Jefferys' Map of General Abercromby's unsuccessful attack on Ticonderoga in 1758. (Clements Library, University of Michigan.)

could have used at least fifty Indians fanning out ahead, but he had only eight.

A quarter of a mile behind Gage came St. Clair's pioneers hacking out a roadway for the gun carriages and a few wagons. Behind them another quarter of a mile was the main body, the wagons, and a herd of cattle just crossing the ford.

The French at Fort Duquesne had known of the English approach for days but were undecided whether to attack them en route or rely on the strength of their fort with its fifteen cannon. Their Indian allies were mercurial in their offers of aid. On some days there were as many as sixteen hundred French and Indians milling around the fort under Captain Contrecœur. Savage parties were sent out to harass Braddock, but his concentrated column discouraged them. Plans to strike the enemy some delaying blow materialized only on July 9, when Captain Daniel de Beaujeu started out with two hundred and ninety regulars and milita and more than six hundred Indians—Ottawas, Chippewas, Potawatomis, Mingos, Shawnees, etc. They collided unexpectedly with the redcoats. Gage heard musket fire ahead, and his scouts came running back. The vanguard formed a skirmish line and opened fire on the approaching enemy. Captain de Beaujeu and two junior officers were instantly killed, and many of the Canadians ran off. But Captain Jean Dumas assumed command and with quick thinking divided his force, sending them running down the ravines on either side of the British.

Hindsight now indicates that if Gage had pushed forward he could have broken through the thin opposition ahead, gained the clear ground, and brought the enemy into the open. But he did not know the strength of the French directly in front, so he retreated. In falling back he found himself running a gauntlet of cross fire from the French and Indians in the ravines and from those who had gained the hilltop he had neglected to guard.

Hearing the rising intensity of the musketry, Braddock ordered Lieutenant Colonel Ralph Burton ahead with eight hundred men. This detachment was soon thrown into confusion when it was overrun by Gage's troops retreating on a rumor that the Indians had gained their rear. The men milled around the narrow roadway bunched together, presenting excellent targets for the enemy. The British could rarely see even one Frenchman or Indian, but the bullets stung them fatally. There is some evidence for thinking that a few of the Indians possessed rifles. Braddock rode up with his aides and tried to get the troops to move forward or at least to form into firing lines. His shouts went unheeded, he struck out with the flat of his sword, and five times his mount was shot from under him. The pandemonium of the milling soldiers, yelling Indians, crying wounded, and the cracking muskets, accented by an occasional cannon roar, heralded disaster. Washington asked for orders to lead an attack on the vital hill, but Braddock shook his head in confusion. Then the general fell wounded.

Colonel Halkett, in charge of the rear, stupidly moved forward and wedged against the desperate troops. He was promptly killed, along with young Shirley. The battle lasted three hours. Of the eighty-six officers present, sixty-three were killed or wounded. All attempts to rally the men into attacking parties failed. They began to flee back toward the river ford. Burton tried to stop them but found it impossible. Of the fourteen hundred and fifty troops almost a thousand were wounded or killed. The enemy apparently suffered fewer than sixty casualties.

Washington found a cart to carry Braddock, and the once-confident column turned back on its trail, leaving more than four hundred and fifty men on the bloody roadway. Braddock whispered orders to Washington to ride ahead to Dunbar's camp, fifty miles away, and send up food and wagons for the wounded. As he passed the fugitive soldiers, many of them walking wounded, Washington was surprised to overtake Gage, who was once again at the head of the reversed expedition. "We have been most scandalously beaten by a trifling body of men," was Washington's summary of the battle.

The survivors streamed into Dunbar's camp (east of Uniontown) on July 11 and 12. Braddock died the next day, and Washington buried him in the road so that the Indians would not discover his grave. Dunbar now commanded and might have stopped at the Great Meadows until reinforced. He still had an army of fifteen hundred, but he burned his wagons and baggage and hurried back to Fort Cumberland, proposing to go into winter quarters at Philadelphia—in July!

Braddock's defeat stunned Virginia. Governor Dinwiddie hastened to offer four to five hundred militia to Dunbar if he would make a second attempt on Fort Duquesne, but Dunbar had had enough. Virginia, Maryland, and Pennsylvania were now left unprotected from hostile Indians and French on their western borders.

While Braddock was marching westward into the jaws of defeat, Admiral Edward Boscawen was cruising off Louisbourg and failing in his mission. He had been sent out with thirteen ships to intercept French reinforcements that everyone knew were going to Canada. By attacking in American waters, the British naïvely hoped to postpone formal war with France. When the first French ships came in sight on June 8, Captain Richard Howe managed to capture two transports containing ten companies of regulars. But the rest of Admiral de la Motte's fleet, hidden by fog, got safely into Louisbourg or Quebec with sixty-eight companies. Boscawen sailed into Halifax, from which port he set up a blockade to bottle up the French ships. Again he was outmaneuvered when the ships at Quebec escaped by taking the perilous course around the north side of Newfoundland through fog and icebergs. Later the ships at Louisbourg made a run for the open sea and only one was lost to the British.

Braddock's death made Governor Shirley commander in chief. The news reached him while he was in the midst of pushing the two other expeditions in New York: one aimed at Niagara under his personal command, the other pointed toward Crown Point under William Johnson as a temporary major general. Shirley ordered Colonel Dunbar to accept Governor Dinwiddie's offer of additional militia and make a second thrust at Fort Duquesne *unless* he felt his regulars were too demoralized to proceed. With this much option, Dunbar seized upon the excuse and followed Shirley's alternative command to march his troops to Albany.

Johnson, who had been appointed superintendent of northern Indian affairs by Braddock, obtained support from the Iroquois after a council lasting from June 24 to July 4. He had conceived an amphibious operation up the Hudson fifty miles from Albany, overland fifteen miles to Lake George, then down that lake to Lake Champlain and Crown Point, erecting three forts along the way. About thirty-five hundred New

England and New York troops were raised for him, all of them raw and with only one engineer, plus about four hundred Indians. Phineas Lyman, Yale 1738, Connecticut legislator, and second in command, started up river in the middle of July with a thousand men. The second division of twelve hundred and the artillery left at the end of the month. Johnson set off from Albany with the third division on August 9.

Fort Edward, a supply depot, was the first fort built by General Lyman. Leaving some men there, Johnson and Lyman marched across the hills to the head of Lake George and commenced a second fort. Thus were the divided forces found by the French early in September. Governor the Marquis de Vaudreuil-Cavagnal, the same who had been governor of Louisiana and eldest son of the old Governor Vaudreuil, had arrived at his new capital, Quebec, on June 26, along with Baron Dieskau, a German in the French service. The latter had been ordered to take the offensive against Fort Oswego on Lake Ontario. Guessing at Johnson's objective, however, Vaudreuil ordered Dieskau to Fort St. Frédéric instead.

On September 1, Dieskau took thirty-two hundred French and Indians out of Crown Point to block the advance of the English. Misled by an English prisoner, he decided to strike at Fort Edward with only fifteen hundred men. On the way he learned of the English forces at Lake George, largely unprotected by fortifications, and turned aside to attack them. Johnson's Indians found the tracks of the Frenchmen, and early on September 8 Johnson foolishly sent off a thousand men under Colonel Ephraim Williams (for whom Williams College was afterward named) and Chief Hendrick to attack. Shrewd old Hendrick observed of the detachment: "If they are to be killed, too many; if they are to fight, too few."

The roles of Braddock and Beaujeu were now reversed: the professional French officer fashioned an ambuscade to entrap the provincial force. It worked, because Colonel Williams failed to put out advance or flanking scouts. His negligence cost him his life and Hendrick's in the first volley; his men panicked and fled back to camp. Johnson rallied seventeen hundred effectives behind breastworks and cannon as the pursuing Frenchmen came in sight. He was wounded in the first exchange of fire, and Lyman directed the defense. Many of the French officers were shot down, including Captain St. Pierre of Fort Le Bœuf, and the Canadians and Indians began to ravel away at the edges. Lyman ordered a sortie that caused the enemy to retreat four miles and left the wounded Dieskau to be captured while sitting alone on a stump.

Toward dusk the resting French force was surprised by Captain McGinnis and two hundred militia going from Fort Edward toward Johnson. McGinnis was killed, but the militia drove the Frenchmen from their ground, killed many in the process, and captured their baggage. Thus the weary enemy had experienced three engagements in one day, winning the first, breaking off the second, and definitely losing the third. Yet the English suffered more casualties—262 to 230. As nominal commander of the victorious side, Johnson was knighted, made a baronet, and confirmed by the Crown in his position as superintendent of Indian affairs in the North. He remained at Lake George to finish Fort William Henry and revealed a surprising lack of control over garrison troops. Many of them refused to work on the fort unless paid extra, and there was considerable insubordination. An advance on Crown Point was forgotten. In November, Johnson wrote to Shirley that he must devote himself to administrative duties with the Indians and gave up his military commission. His force was reduced to garrisons for the two northern forts.

The French forces remained at Crown Point and even planned another fort ten miles farther south, where Lake George outlets into Lake Champlain. The spot carried an Indian name of Ticonderoga.

Shirley had not been nearly so successful as Johnson, in the eyes of London. With a smaller force—his and Pepperrell's new regiments, a thousand Massachusetts and New Jersey militia, totaling twenty-four hundred—he had moved westward from Albany toward the end of July. His authority and activity in New York had aroused the jealousy of Lieutenant Governor James Delancey, a small-time, ambitious politician, particularly after Shirley urged him to stop the contraband trade between Albany and Montreal. The local traders involved were Delancey's political supporters. Further, when Shirley asked Johnson to procure a hundred Indian guides for him, Johnson became ruffled and, abetted by Delancey, procrastinated and then refused.

Despite this lack of co-operation Shirley was not easily discouraged. He had sent Captain John Bradstreet with part of Pepperrell's regiment to Fort Oswego late in May, with shipwrights to begin four vessels for Lake Ontario. He had found boatmen to handle his enormous transportation problem in and out of rivers on the 250-mile route, and he had finally obtained a promise of a hundred Indians to meet him as Oswego for the descent on Fort Niagara. The New Jersey contingent was put in motion, and Shirley followed it slowly with seventeen hundred men. The artillery came behind. Everyone reached Oswego safely by September 2.

Since the French had twelve hundred men at Fort Frontenac,

only fifty miles away, ready to move against Oswego or to reinforce Niagara, Shirley set about strengthening his Lake Ontario base by constructing a second fort of logs on the hill across the river's mouth. His plan to push on to Niagara was delayed first by rains, then by sickness, and finally by the failure of provisions to arrive before the restless Indians began to desert. A council of officers on September 27 favored postponing the attack until spring. Reluctantly Shirley acceded and posted his and Pepperrell's regiments as garrison troops. The militia returned eastward, as did Shirley late in October. He tried to stir Johnson to continue on to Crown Point and received his resignation instead.

As commander in chief he still insisted on assuming the offensive. In the conference he called for December, 1755, with Governor Hardy (newly appointed to New York), Governors Sharpe of Maryland, Morris of Pennsylvania, and Fitch of Connecticut, and Colonels Dunbar and St. Clair, he proposed to assemble six thousand men at Oswego to proceed against Niagara in the spring. Ten thousand men were to be sought to take Crown Point, three thousand to retrace Braddock's route to Fort Duquesne, and still another force to row up the Kennebec River in a feint against Quebec. These were ambitious and costly plans, involving more soldiers than had heretofore been dreamed of. Virginia, Maryland, and Pennsylvania would not support a second attempt on Fort Duquesne and definitely were not interested in a campaign against faraway Crown Point. They preferred a defense posture and recommended that the regiments of regulars take Niagara (at Crown expense), which would force a withdrawal of the French from Duquesne. Disappointed, Shirley returned to Boston, leaving orders—never carried out—to forward provisions to Oswego.

This division of viewpoints was not auspicious for Shirley and came after Delancey had undermined him in correspondence with England. Regardless of Shirley's innocence or weakness or deviousness, the Board of Trade recommended to the cabinet that for the sake of harmony another commander in chief from England should be sent to America. The perspective of time suggests that Shirley possessed too much energy and drive for the jealous governors and penny-pinching assemblies. He was also impatient of military accounting and paperwork, and here his subordinates could take profitable advantage of him. At the same time, this extraordinary civilian had better military judgment than Britain could uncover in the first three commanders in chief sent here from the career officer corps. As Benjamin Franklin reflected on him, he "was sensible and sagacious in himself, and attentive to good Advice from others, capable of forming judicious Plans, quick and active in carrying them into Execution." As one example, he had organized a company of woodsmen from New Hampshire as Rangers, under Captain Robert Rogers. They were to do scouting, bring in prisoners for information, and generally serve as the eyes and ears of the regular forces. The innovation eventually reformed the British army.

In March, 1756, the British ministry ordered Shirley to London, after he had turned over his command to John Campbell, the Earl of Loudoun, an experienced Scottish officer, fifty-one years old, short, ill-tempered, and unimaginative. Able he might be, but facing the difficulties incident to command in America, he accomplished little.

After all the year's warlike activity—four battles between the soldiers and sailors of two nations legally at peace—England finally declared war on France May 18, 1756. Newcastle had not wanted war but felt bound to protect the English colonies which he deemed to have been invaded by the French. He may have hoped to fight a limited war and found it impossible. Peace in Europe depended on England's subsidizing of certain German states, while opposition to this policy increased rapidly. The declaration of war was made just two days before the English and French fleets met over the latter's attempt to seize Minorca. After the battle the English withdrew to Gibraltar, and Minorca fell to France, which accepted the state of war. Generally known now as the French and Indian War (as if the others had not happened), it was at the time of the American Revolution called simply "the French War" and the earlier King George's War was termed "the Old French War."

In Europe the conflict became known simply as the Seven Years' War. Prussia and Austria changed sides. Because England would not help Maria Theresa recover Silesia, she joined France and posed a threat to Hanover. England welcomed Frederick of Prussia as an ally to protect Hanover and threaten France; he had already insulted Louis XV by naming his lap dog "Madame de Pompadour." Russia, Poland, Sweden, and Saxony joined France and Austria, making a combined population of ninety million people. England, Prussia, and Hanover could tally only twelve million. The population proportion was reversed in America, where the English colonies could boast of a million and a quarter inhabitants as against about seventy-five thousand in Canada and Louisiana. It was truly a world war, with battles in Europe, America, the West Indies, Africa, India, and the Philippines.

In America the plan of defense created by the ministry and the Duke of Cumberland had failed. The colonial assemblies had never voted a common defense fund, they had failed to provide sufficient wagons or provisions or enough recruits to join British regiments. The economy sought by the ministry was impossible, and Braddock's expedition was supported almost completely from London. Contrary to original plans, the northern colonies had raised a wholly American army of seven thousand by the energy of General Shirley. Moreover, the only battle won had been fought by these militia. It was clear that the American provinces were not going to co-operate with regular British forces except on their own terms.

The previous colonial wars were largely echoes of European conflicts which had started first. Now in the final struggle for empire, hostilities began in America and spread slowly to the home countries. What made this war even more significant was the viewpoint of William Pitt, who came to have the management of it as secretary of state. He held the new and strange conviction that France could be best reduced in power and influence by taking away her colonies rather than by trying for the fourth time to defeat her big army at home. Consequently, the focus of the war was now outside the continent, with a kind of holding operation in Europe by the Prussian and British armies and especially by the British navy.

VIII

Royal Americans and Rangers

Seven Yrs war

The war was not going favorably for England and her colonies, and for another year it continued to be a harvest of defeats and disappointments. The English had won in Nova Scotia and repelled an invasion at Lake George. They had failed to prevent reinforcements from reaching Canada, had lost Minorca, and had been routed before Fort Duquesne. Holding the Great Lakes and Ohio Valley as well as the Mississippi, the French were in the ascendency, and General Loudoun was not the man to reverse the course of events.

Since earlier arrangements for joint military endeavor with the colonies under Braddock had been disappointing, the ministry revised the amount of co-operation to be required. Two more regiments of regulars were coming to America, the Thirty-fifth and the Forty-second, their depleted ranks hopefully to be filled out here. In addition, an enormous new regiment of four battalions of one thousand men each was to be raised in America and paid from London. In this way Americans would be enlisted in the regular army but would serve together. The officers were to be professionals but not necessarily English; several Swiss officers were available for service, and Americans might look forward to promotion. The regiment was called the Royal Americans and numbered the Sixty-second, later the Sixtieth. It continues in existence today.

Militia were still to be used in a secondary capacity, although the Crown did not like their temporary nature or disciplinary vagaries. The colonial assemblies tried to maintain absolute control of the forces they raised, and they were asked to help in recruiting with bounties and to send provisions to Albany. Thereafter the Crown would feed the provincial troops, and the officers learned they must obey British officers of the rank of major and above.

Command of His Majesty's enlarged forces in North America was vested in Lieutenant General Loudoun and two major generals: James Abercromby and Daniel Webb. Unfortunately, the increase in quantity was not matched by any rise in quality. Abercromby was Loudoun's age and a close friend. An undistinguished officer who could carry out orders much better than he could originate them, he owed his appointment largely to political gratitude from Newcastle. Webb, six years older than his two colleagues, was a former cavalry officer selected by Cumberland for a role beyond his capacity. He was cautious, lacking in self-confidence and judgment, and soon incapacitated by palsy.

The war and navy offices were incredibly slow in getting transports ready, so Loudoun did not embark until May 20, 1756, with his aide, two secretaries, his mistress, and seventeen servants. He reached New York on July 23. Abercromby and Webb had preceded him by a month to prepare an offensive campaign for the summer. They found arrangements under Shirley in great confusion and ignored his warning to reinforce Oswego at once. Upon arrival Loudoun quietly canceled his plan to attack Crown Point with militia.

In contrast, the French minister of war had selected the Marquis de Montcalm to command the troops in Canada and dispatched him with two battalions (twelve hundred men) on April 3. They reached Quebec by the middle of May. Montcalm was forty-four and, like his opponents, a veteran of the previous war. Unlike them, he was resourceful and dashing—even impetuous. For the second and third in command he was assigned the Chevaliers de Lévis and de Bourlamaque. Brigadier François Gaston de Lévis was thirty-six and had been an officer for twenty years, his competence a dependable joy. Colonel François Charles de Bourlamaque was an engineer who had served also as governor of Guadeloupe. Unfortunately, Montcalm was officially subordinate to the Canadian governor, the Marquis de Vaudreuil-Cavagnal. Canadian-born Vaudreuil was egotistical yet indecisive under stress, and was jealous of officers from France.

Promptly Montcalm and Lévis paid a visit to the upper part of Lake Champlain to inspect Fort Carillon then being built at Ticonderoga. It represented a stronger and deeper arrow into New York than Crown Point. Lévis remained as commandant, while Montcalm turned his attention to Lake Ontario. He learned that the two American regiments at Fort Oswego had suffered the loss of scores of men during the winter from disease and desertion. From Fort Frontenac (Kingston, Ontario), Montcalm easily took the unfinished fort on August 13 when the English abandoned it and the old one by cannonade the following day. The commandant and eighty others were killed, including some by French Indians after the surrender. It was ominous that Montcalm could not control his red allies. The Fiftieth and Fifty-first regiments passed out of existence, although they were reconstituted in England. Bourlamaque was left in command at Frontenac. With Fort Niagara at the other end, Ontario was now completely a French lake.

This initial setback prompted Loudoun to call for militia reinforcements from the assemblies of New England, New York, and New Jersey. Like Braddock, he insisted on proper discipline, assured supplies, and all the apparatus attending a European army before he would move into action. The colonies showed themselves to be as wary of him as they were of the French. All evaded his request. Not unreasonably the aristocratic Loudoun soon came to feel that the British army in America must be independent of provincial aid or obligation. Virginia was slowly strengthening its ravaged frontier with militia under George Washington, a colonel once more. At Winchester, Fort Loudoun was built, and sixteen other blockhouses were spaced through the back country. Southern Indians were finally persuaded to furnish warriors for protection against the northern tribes. In similar fashion Pennsylvania was forced to guard its western and northern flanks by a series of sixteen posts garrisoned by militia.

No campaign was planned for late 1756. Instead, Loudoun concentrated on raising forces to assault Quebec the following year. Briefly, he planned to take north fifty-five hundred regulars—four regiments and two battalions of the Sixtieth. They would be supported by a fleet from England. He would leave the Thirty-fifth, a battalion of the Sixtieth, and four Independent Companies in New York to serve, with five thousand militia, as a defensive force—a total of sixty-seven hundred and fifty men—under Webb. In the South the other battalion of the Sixtieth and some provincials would stand guard. Having revealed that he wanted four thousand troops from the four New England provinces, Loudoun was met by four different quota proposals. In the end the colonies accepted the commander's figures, but none of the troops was ready on the promised date of March 25, 1757. Although Loudoun found the other governors more tractable, their assemblies were not. The southern colonies procrastinated, and Pennsylvania and Maryland failed him altogether. New Jersey provided half the men requested, and only New York came through on time. Despite all these difficulties and delays, he at last achieved some military union among the colonies. For the first time the commander in chief was able to post troops where he wanted them along the frontier. He also increased Rogers' Rangers to a corps of several companies, paid as an adjunct to the regulars. So far, so good.

Back in England, meanwhile, William Pitt had come to power in December, 1756, and ousted the men who had appointed Loudoun. This did not mean his recall, or less interest in the war in America. On the contrary! Pitt was not only convinced that England's prestige and power rested on her colonies, which must be increased rather than lost, but he also insisted, "I am sure I can save this country, and nobody else can." Vain and disagreeable such a man might be, but this one built his conceit on undeniable talents. He was honest to a degree not previously seen in government. He believed his country should be served by its ablest men and that he could recognize them. He was energetic to the point of impatience and, again, convinced that France could be humbled by seizing her colonies rather

than by facing her huge army on Europe's hard-packed battle-
fields. To achieve victory, he was not afraid to spend money,
thus overcoming the chief colonial objection to co-operation.
Nor was he reluctant to impose his will on the commander in
chief in America. Indeed, one of his first decisions was to order
Loudoun to take Louisbourg before attempting Quebec and to
send him large reinforcements for that purpose.

Dutifully Loudoun changed his objective and tardily embarked his regulars from New York on May 21 for Halifax. Ten
regiments coming from Ireland left only on May 8 for the same
port. The delay permitted a fleet of twenty-two French ships to
get to Louisbourg first to strengthen the garrison of twenty-
five hundred. The English contingents made Halifax by June 30
and found themselves immobilized by fog and contrary winds
throughout July. They also had no exact information on the
force at Louisbourg. Finally, on August 4 as they were at last
ready to embark, the navy learned from a captured French
vessel that the enemy's naval strength was greater than that of
the English. Vice-Admiral Francis Holbourne told Loudoun
that his expedition was hopeless, but Loudoun made the final
decision to abandon his attempt and return to New York. A
month later Holbourne's fleet was crippled by a hurricane and
only part of it returned to England. The weather was indubi-
tably against the expedition, but some doubt remains whether
the circumstances should have prevented action. The result
disgusted Pitt and encouraged him to exert more control of the
military so as not to permit discretion on the part of commanders. Franklin called the campaign "frivolous, expensive
and disgraceful to our Nation beyond Conception."

More than mere failure to take a fort resulted from this affair. The long absence of the regulars, isolated from **action, en-**

couraged Montcalm to assume the offensive. Governor Vaudreuil earlier had planned to capture Fort William Henry and Fort Edward. In March he had even sent his brother, Rigaud de Vaudreuil, as leader of an expedition against Fort William Henry at the head of Lake George, but it had failed. Montcalm now prepared to move south from Fort Ticonderoga. With about six thousand troops and two thousand Indians he approached Fort William Henry in August. Lévis was with him as well as his aide, Colonel Louis de Bougainville, a scholarly young officer, while the Abbé Picquet and three other priests shepherded the Indians.

Webb was at Fort Edward on the Hudson with 3,400 men; Lieutenant Colonel George Munro of the Thirty-fifth Regiment commanded at Fort William Henry with 1,300. The French had already captured 250 provincials out on a scouting mission in July. These figures total 4,950 out of 6,750 men on paper. Where were the others? If they existed, they must have been distributed at Albany and up the Mohawk. Even after learning of Montcalm's preparations and obvious objective, Webb did not move up in force or call in time on the colonies for the additional militia available for emergencies.

Montcalm's forces came in sight of Fort William Henry on August 2. That day eight hundred men from Fort Edward came in, the only reinforcement Webb made. Munro's fort would not hold five hundred men; the others lay in an entrenched camp half a mile away. The siege began next day, with both sides cannonading. On the seventh Montcalm sent in by a flag of truce a captured letter to Munro from Webb that said the writer could offer no further support until the new militia came in, and if they didn't come, "you might be able to make the best Terms left in your power." Munro had suffered only one hundred and thirty killed and wounded, although all his cannon had burst. But the Massachusetts militia, feeling abandoned, told their colonel they were going home. A council of officers on August 9, discouraged by the letter, advised Munro to surrender, and he did. Montcalm allowed the men to keep their baggage, arms, and horses. They were to march out the next morning and be escorted to Fort Edward on their word not to serve again for eighteen months.

Disappointed in their anticipation of plunder, the Indian allies of the French began boldly to strip the British and Americans of their packs, in which they found brandy. The French guards merely advised the prisoners to submit. Other Indians were coolly butchering the eighty-seven sick and wounded, and this massacre panicked some of the soldiers into running off. The Indians eagerly pursued them and scalped those they caught. Other soldiers and officers implored the French for protection, which was grudgingly and reluctantly given. Montcalm came running to the scene and shouted at his Indians. In the midst of the killing he reputedly bared his breast and cried: "Since you are rebellious children who break the promise you have given to your father and who will not listen to his voice, kill him first of all!"

The French officers finally restored some order. About two hundred prisoners had been killed; another two hundred were carried off northward by the recalcitrant Indians, who now abandoned the French. The rest of the prisoners, approximately sixteen hundred, stayed in the French camp for five days while the victors carried off provisions and burned the fort. Then they marched to Fort Edward. Montcalm made no attempt against that place. The shameful French performance hardened the conviction of New Englanders that papists and savages were leagued in evil. Webb's reputation was ruined when Munro vented his fury before he died in November.

There was bad news in Europe, too. The Duke of Cumberland had met defeat in Germany and resigned in disgrace from the army. At least Pitt was relieved of his hovering presence in military decisions.

Loudoun brought most of his army back to New York on September 1, hopeful of accomplishing something before winter. He considered a siege of Fort Ticonderoga, laid it aside, then took it up again in October and gave it over to Lord Howe, colonel in the Fifty-fifth Regiment, who had joined him at Halifax. The planning failed for want of snowshoes, sleighs, and ice cleats.

The French were not as inactive. Early in November, Ensign Picoté de Bellestre and the Sieur de Lorimer, with three hundred regulars plus as many Canadians and Indians, moved eastward from Lake Ontario to Fort Herkimer, a three-story stone house surrounded by a ditch and palisades, on the south side of the Mohawk River. It was garrisoned by two hundred men of the Twenty-second Regiment under Captain Philip Townshend. But the French force avoided the fort and burst upon the German Flats, a large Palatine settlement on the north bank (Herkimer, New York). These farmers were completely surprised, inasmuch as they had entered into a secret agreement of neutrality with the French and regarded the fort as the only legitimate object of attack. Consequently they had refused Captain Townshend's warning and his orders to come into the fort. They protested bitterly as the French and Indians went about burning their houses and barns, slaughtering and stealing their cattle. Fifty scalps were taken too, and a hundred and fifty prisoners marched off, while hundreds were left impoverished,

bereaved, and homeless. Townshend dared not interfere against
superior numbers, while the Germans learned the futility of
local neutrality.

As the year 1757 came to a close, the French remained in
ascendency. Except for Nova Scotia they had avenged their
defeat at Lake George by completely razing Fort William
Henry. They were squeezing New York from the west as well
as the north, and their control of the Ohio Valley was no longer
challenged. Governor Vaudreuil was laying bold plans for 1758.
Montcalm was to move down to Lake George again and seize
Fort Edward. Lévis was to take three thousand men into the
Iroquois country and so impress the Indians with French might
that they would join him in sweeping down the Mohawk.
Albany would be doomed.

The only deterrent to these plans was food. Two successive
bad harvests, the capture of sixteen provisions ships coming
from France the previous summer, and thirty-five hundred
more regulars from home to feed had already limited the inhabitants of Quebec to four ounces of bread and a little salt
pork per day. By the next spring the ration would be cut in
half, with no supply ships from France expected before June.
This necessity of waiting for ships from home to provide any
expeditionary force with the required food delayed campaigns
and thereby shortened the season of offensive activity.

But William Pitt could plan, too. On December 30, 1757, he
ordered Loudoun to turn over his command to Abercromby
and return to England. At the same time he asked the northern
governors to raise at least twenty thousand men to join the
king's forces in an invasion of Canada by way of Crown Point;
southern governors were called upon to furnish several thousand men for further operations. Further, these provincial troops

would be equipped and fed at the king's expense, their officers would rank next to regulars having similar rank, and as for other expenses falling on the colonies he would urge Parliament to reimburse them. These concessions to colonial desires were a tremendous inducement to military exertion. Regular regiments would be kept up to strength by sending out recruits from England. In addition, there would be militia for temporary service at local expense. Later Pitt designated the objectives he had in mind: an "irruption into Canada," an amphibious operation against Louisbourg again, and another march on Fort Duquesne. He was anticipating employment of twenty-four thousand regulars and twenty-five thousand provincials, and he was committing Great Britain to a huge war debt. But the French would feel his muscle.

Most of the regular regiments in America were to be utilized against Louisbourg, but with the remaining units and the provincials Abercromby was to invade Canada by way of Lake Champlain. He was also to detach Brigadier General John Forbes to lead military operations in the southern colonies. Abercromby set about preparing for the thousands of provincials and moving up to Lake George the regulars, Independent Companies, and Rangers amounting to about sixty-five hundred. The colonies fell down on their quotas and fewer than ten thousand men were on hand July 4, 1758, when the combined army of sixteen thousand took to the water and rowed down the lake. Nine hundred bateaux, one hundred and thirty-five whale boats, and rafts of artillery covered the width of the lake and extended for several miles, as colorful a military spectacle as the war had seen. They landed in a cove on the west side of Lake George, a few miles from Fort Ticonderoga, on the night of July 5–6.

Royal Americans and Rangers

By this time, food from France having arrived only in the middle of June, Montcalm had barely been able to get troops down to Ticonderoga. The fort could not hold more than a few hundred, so he set his men to digging entrenchments well in front of the fort and building an abatis, or barrier of fallen trees. The trunks lay parallel, the tree tops pointing toward the enemy, and many of the branches were denuded of leaves and sharpened. This entanglement of slashings rose higher than a man and was a hundred yards in depth. It extended across the small peninsula from the narrows of Lake Champlain to the outlet of Lake George. As a further asset, Montcalm had Lévis to command the right wing and Bourlamaque the left. Still, he was extremely vulnerable: he was outnumbered almost five to one; the English had cannon with them, about forty pieces; and just south of Ticonderoga rose a lofty hill, now called Mount Defiance, that commanded the fort.

Once the English had landed, an advance force under Lord Howe plunged into the woods early on July 6. It unexpectedly collided with a French reconnaissance force and routed it, killing a hundred and seizing about one hundred and fifty prisoners. But the English lost two hundred and thirty wounded and eighty-seven killed, among them Lord Howe, the popular second in command. Universally respected as he was and supplying the fighting dash that Abercromby lacked, Howe's death punctured the spirit of the whole army. No other brigadiers were available, and no colonels of his caliber. General Lyman, who commanded the other wing, was a provincial and lacked Howe's personality. Colonel Thomas Gage, of Monongahela fame, became second in command. He had organized a regiment of light infantry modeled after Major Rogers' Rangers.

Abercromby pushed his men forward again on the seventh

and made two fatal errors of judgment. One was to believe the reports of the French prisoners that Montcalm had six thousand men (where could he have put them?) and was imminently expecting three thousand more—hence, a direct assault must be made quickly. The other, proceeding from the assumed need for speed, was to ignore his cannon, which, had he put them on top of Mount Defiance, would have made the fort uninhabitable. Instead, he sent Superintendent Johnson and his Indians up there. Their muskets had no effect, and the only advantage they gained was an unsurpassed gallery seat for viewing the battle below.

Early on the morning of July 8, Abercromby summoned a council of war limited to deciding how best to carry out the frontal attack. There was no best way without cannon, which could have sent shells over the abatis or cut a path through it or set it on fire with hot shot. Abercromby favored the regulars for the assault, supported by the Massachusetts men, with the other provincials in reserve. His wishes prevailed.

The battle opened about 12:30 P.M., with Rangers, Gage's light infantry, and Bradstreet's bateau men driving in the outposts. Then wave after wave of redcoats threw themselves against the tree barrier and were shot down as they tried to penetrate the tangle of branches. Fires that did start among the slashings were put out by the French. The Forty-second Regiment almost disappeared as it suffered two hundred and three killed and almost three hundred wounded. Six advances were ordered in mad pursuit of Abercromby's fixed idea. Changing the particular points of pressure did no good, for the abatis could not be pierced under fire.

At 7:00 P.M. the assault was finally halted, and withdrawal began. Total losses were four hundred and sixty-four killed, eleven hundred and seventeen wounded, and twenty-nine missing—10 per cent of the English force. Throughout the night the weary men stumbled through the woods toward their boats. Abercromby's mistakes had led inevitably to the debacle.

The French were not only exhausted but uneasy. They had suffered about four hundred casualties, and Bourlamaque was severely wounded. Surely the English would resume the attack in the morning, this time with their cannon. Such overwhelming strength would carry the day. Montcalm made plans for retreat down the lake as far as St. Jean on the Richelieu River.

But next morning the redcoats were gone!—afloat on Lake George back to Fort Edward. Montcalm was overjoyed. The French had won again. Except for Dieskau's rout after three engagements in one day back in 1755, the French had rolled over the English ever since 1754. Well might they celebrate. Their invincibility, however, would last only eighteen days longer before the wheel of fortune turned.

On July 26, 1758, Louisbourg fell!

Pitt had erred in appointing Abercromby to succeed Loudoun and then in taking away most of his regulars, forcing him to delay his expedition against Ticonderoga while waiting for provincials. But Pitt had formulated a concomitant stroke that showed his genius. To carry out his plan he did not hesitate to select three colonels who had been fighting in Europe. One was Jeffery Amherst, a forty-one-year-old career officer who had shown great steadiness and reliability although he had never held an independent command. Pitt made him commander of the expedition against Louisbourg with the rank of major general. To assist him, Pitt conferred the rank of brigadier on Colonel James Wolfe, only thirty-one, who had distinguished himself in fighting in spite of being a thin, chinless, sickly man with

The Colonial Wars

a fondness for poetry; on Colonel Edward Whitmore, a veteran of the last war who had headed a regiment for only a few months; and on Governor Charles Lawrence of Nova Scotia, who knew Cape Breton Island intimately. As admirals, Pitt chose Edward Boscawen and Sir Charles Hardy, admonishing them on the absolute necessity of co-operation with the army.

Hardy sailed for Halifax at the end of January, 1758, to prevent a French fleet from entering Louisbourg. Boscawen embarked from Ireland in February with Wolfe and Whitmore aboard; two regiments, and military stores preceded him. Upon their tardy arrival at Halifax in May, they found most of the regiments from Abercromby's command. Hardy had not been completely successful, for eight French ships had swung into Louisbourg behind him.

The expedition—nine thousand regulars and five hundred colonials—got under way from Halifax, according to Pitt's instructions, on May 28, before Amherst's arrival. But en route to Cape Breton, the commander's ship joined the fleet. Amherst decided that the whole force should land at Gabarus Bay, west of Louisbourg, the same plan chosen by the New Englanders in 1745. Because of fog the debarkation was delayed until June 8. The French had thrown up a chain of earthworks, with cannon, around the bay. The elderly Colonel de St. Julhien commanded the two to three thousand regulars, provincials, and Indians who manned these shore defenses. They fought off the first attempt to land, but one boatload of Wolfe's division secured a foothold on a rocky protrusion far to the west. Wolfe turned all his boats on this point while Whitmore and Lawrence were threatening to land at two other spots in the bay. In the confusion Wolfe got his men ashore. St. Julhien sent some troops against the British, but they were thrown back and the battery

The Marquis de Montcalm. From a nineteenth-century engraving; original unknown.

General Sir Jeffery Amherst, age 51. From a portrait by Sir Joshua Reynolds, 1768. (National Gallery of Canada.)

that could play on the enemy was captured. Whitmore and Lawrence now rowed to Wolfe's landing, and the French began pulling back into the Louisbourg defense lines. Wearily the British established a permanent camp on the bay, three miles from the walled town. Wolfe marched twelve hundred men around to Lighthouse Point, east of the town, and occupied the whole northeast shore while erecting a battery.

The French were prepared to endure a siege. Governor de Drucour commanded the troops: three thousand soldiers, twenty-six hundred sailors and marines, and local militia amounting to more than six thousand. Ships' crews had joined the land forces, not without protest, but everyone now must share the common fate. The British pushed their siege lines forward until they could throw shells, hot shot, and bombs into the town. After the hospital was struck on July 6, the defenders realized they must try a determined sortie. A thousand ventured out in the darkness of July 9 and penetrated the front lines, but they retreated with prisoners as British reinforcements came running up. Since this skirmish resulted in no great damage, the siege continued, with increasing destruction of the town. Three of the anchored ships burned after a shell hit the powder magazine in one of them. Building after building was knocked apart or pulled down. One of the bastions was destroyed, but Drucour hung on. Then Boscawen sent boats into the harbor and took two ships. Only four cannon were still working on the ramparts. On July 26 Drucour raised a white flag.

The soldiers and sailors were ordered to England as prisoners of war. French civilians were to be deported to France. Cape Breton and its dependency, Île St. Jean (Prince Edward Island), passed into British hands once more. The St. Lawrence lay open; the mistake of 1748 was rectified. General Whitmore was installed as commandant, but two years later engineers and miners carefully blew up all the fortifications around the empty town. Only ruins survive.

Capture of Louisbourg was a turning point, militarily and psychologically. Pitt had found commanders who could use the preponderant strength of the English in America. Tumbled from superiority, the French would need not only more men but assured supplies even to maintain a defensive line, which depended in turn on an effective French navy.

IX

Anglo-American Allies

The loss of Louisbourg was no unlucky break in the string of
French victories. Rather it indicated a change of season, the
rising barometer of British strength. Two more blows before
the end of 1758 demonstrated that New France was in ominous
trouble.

The first was a daring stroke from Abercromby's badly
mauled army. Although his provincials were melting away after
the defeat at Ticonderoga, he ordered thirty-six hundred men,
most of them colonials, to reinforce Brigadier General John
Stanwix in building a fort at the Oneida Lake carrying place,
beyond the source of the Mohawk River. Lieutenant Colonel
John Bradstreet commanded them and was given permission,
"if found practicable," also to attack Fort Frontenac at the head
of the St. Lawrence. This latter enterprise lay close to Bradstreet's ambitious heart, and after leaving a few troops with

Stanwix he hurried on westward in August with boats and three thousand men.

Fort Frontenac was supply depot and distributing point between the cities of the St. Lawrence and the posts on the Great Lakes. It was usually filled with military equipment, barrels of salted rations, and clothing. Furs from the western country were often received here, and trade goods for the Indians were stocked. A square fort about three hundred feet long on each side, it was made of stone, with large bastions on each corner. Some thirty cannon were mounted on the walls, and barracks existed for soldiers and officers, along with a chapel, powder magazine, store, etc. Some of the storage barns were located outside the fort. At this moment the garrison amounted to only one hundred and ten men under Captain de Noyan, for Governor Vaudreuil was sure that the English were not active west of Oneida Lake.

Bradstreet moved quickly to the ruins of Oswego and ordered his bateau men to slide their boats into the bay later known as Sackett's Harbor. De Noyan's Indians discovered their presence, and the commandant sent off an express to Montreal for help. Bradstreet's men landed a mile from the fort without opposition on the evening of August 25. Next day they dragged their cannon ashore and pulled them to within 400 yards of the fort. Bombardment was begun and was answered by the French, without much damage to either side. During the night Bradstreet shifted some cannon around to the north side and occupied an old entrenchment only 160 yards from the wall. The shells and balls were much more effective now, and De Noyan hauled down his colors. Bradstreet let the garrison depart on parole, to be exchanged for a like number of English prisoners in Canada. The fort was demolished, seven French ships were burned, and two were loaded with the captured supplies. By September 13 the English force had rejoined General Stanwix at Oneida, and New France had lost not only a fort but control of Lake Ontario.

DUQUESNE

The second blow fell farther south. Brigadier General John Forbes commanded a new expedition against Fort Duquesne to be made up of seventeen hundred regulars and five thousand provincials. Forbes was fifty-one and far from well. He intended to gather his "southern" army at Fort Cumberland and proceed along Braddock's old road. Sir John St. Clair was detached to serve as quartermaster general, as he had for Braddock, and he seems to have persuaded Forbes early in May, 1758, to cut a new road across Pennsylvania from Carlisle. Horses and wagons were more likely to be available here than in western Virginia, and the distance was shorter. But it would take time to construct a new road through the mountains. Colonel Washington was disgusted when he learned of the new route, because the necessary delay and slow movement, he felt, would cause the Indian allies to desert. He was right.

Raystown (modern Bedford) on the frontier was made the base of supplies. The Pennsylvania and Virginia governors and assemblies, ready to help, raised forty-seven hundred men. North Carolina sent three hundred, to replace the Independent Companies from South Carolina that remained at home. The truculent Maryland Assembly did nothing, but since the Crown had been paying a Maryland company to garrison Fort Cumberland, that company was drafted into the expedition. The regulars were simply the Seventy-seventh Regiment and a battalion of the Sixtieth under the remarkable Lieutenant Colonel Henry

Bouquet, a Swiss professional who was Forbes's second in command. Figures on the promised Indians rose and fell each week. Indians—including the Delawares and Shawnees whom Pennsylvania had been cultivating during the past two years in an effort to wean them away from the French—came demanding arms, clothing, and supplies; then they would go off ostensibly to make war on the French. By July most of the southern Indians had tired of Forbes's slowness and had gone home. A few appeared in the fall, pled for expensive presents, got them, and disappeared. Luckily, as matters turned out, Forbes's army did not need Indians.

Bouquet was the officer on the spot who carried out most of Forbes's plans. He contracted for wagons in May, loaded them in June, and was at Raystown by July ready to build a fort —Fort Bedford. He had ordered Colonel Washington to assemble his Virginia regiment at Fort Cumberland and then cut a road north to Raystown. Washington was still pessimistic about the new route and even tried to argue Bouquet out of it. But slashing through the woods, up hill and down dale, the British cut a road westward. By September 3, Colonel James Burd with twenty-five hundred men reached Loyalhanna Creek and began constructing Fort Ligonier, fifty miles beyond Fort Bedford and forty miles from Fort Duquesne. For a few weeks these men could be fed only by rapidly reducing the supplies at Bedford. Failure of wagoners to respond left the Bedford depot dangerously depleted. A threat from Forbes and action by the Pennsylvania Assembly turned more wagons onto the western road so that by October 21 the crisis had passed.

The British now were anxious to see what the French were doing. Bouquet sent Major James Grant of the Seventy-seventh with a mixed detachment of eight hundred and forty to observe

Indian Superintendent Sir William Johnson. Painted after the French and Indian War; artist unknown. (New-York Historical Society.)

William Pitt, age 45. From an engraving of a portrait by William Hoare, 1753. (John Carter Brown Library, Brown University.)

Fort Duquesne only, take some Indian prisoners if possible, and then return. They set out from Ligonier on September 11. Within sight of the French on the fourteenth, all of Grant's plans went awry. He had achieved surprise because there were no Indians east of the fort, but he threw it away by using his drummers to beat an unauthorized advance on the fort. The sound aroused the garrison, and as Grant moved down the hill that bears his name in Pittsburgh, he was met by superior numbers of French and Indians. Grant's rear guard moved forward and missed the retreating vanguard. Separated parties fought bravely or ran away. Grant himself was surrounded and captured. Only five hundred and twenty-five of the detachment returned to Ligonier, eloquent proof that the French under the Sieur de Ligneris were still active.

This setback, however, could not stop the momentum of Forbes's thrust. An attempt by the French and Indians to invade the Ligonier camp on October 12 failed. Moreover, in both engagements the Indians had suffered the greater casualties and they began to lose their zest for this white man's war. Others in their tribes had received invitations to visit the English and make peace. A conference going on at Easton this moment was removing an old complaint of the tribes on the Ohio and thus undermining French influence. The message of conciliation was carried west.

By November 2 the ailing Forbes himself was at Ligonier with five thousand troops. Ten days later the French tried to capture their horses and were chased away. An Englishman who had been captured by the Indians was recovered; he revealed that both the Canadians and many of the Indians had left Duquesne. Although Forbes, suffering painful weakness, could no longer walk or ride, he silenced his officers who wanted to winter at Fort Ligonier and ordered the troops forward. As provincials under Colonel Washington blazed a trail, the rest of the army followed to a camp only a few miles from Fort Duquesne. Forbes was borne on a litter slung between two horses. On the night of November 24 the men heard a tremendous explosion. Next day they came in sight of the smoking ruins of Fort Duquesne, blown up and burned. No enemy was in sight—only a row of grisly stakes erected by the Indians. On each one was the head of one of Grant's detachment and a Scottish kilt tied around its base.

Captain de Ligneris had not taken a cowardly course. The capture of Fort Frontenac required him to send away his Canadians because he could no longer feed them during the winter. Many of them were from the Illinois country. He had about three hundred regulars left. His gamble was that the British might decide to winter at Ligonier—and they nearly did. But when they came on instead, De Ligneris was under orders to destroy his post rather than endure a siege and capture. He pulled back to the fort at Venango, hoping he would be able to advance again in the spring. The upper Ohio Valley passed into English hands, another crack in the French empire.

The dying Forbes left the Ohio forks on December 4. Lieutenant Colonel Hugh Mercer, a Pennsylvania physician, was put in command of a garrison encamped there and soon was examining sites for a new fort to be named for William Pitt. The other forts across the province were garrisoned for the winter, and a steady flow of provisions by pack horse was maintained, chiefly by the energy of Colonel Bouquet. The new Indian friends of the British on the Ohio also expected to be fed. They were relieved that the general had marched away with most of his army, they looked forward to trade with the English, and they promised to bring in their English captives. General Forbes was carried back to Philadelphia, where he died on March 11, 1759.

In the same month that Fort Duquesne was abandoned to the British, General Abercromby received notice from Pitt of his recall. The Ticonderoga fiasco was too much for the impatient minister, whereas the victor at Louisbourg showed promise. Amherst had sailed to Boston with most of his regiments in September, 1758, and then marched to Lake George. Abercromby turned over the command to him, probably with relief.

Enjoying wide popularity at home, Pitt was virtually autonomous in prosecuting the war. The European theater was satisfactory in fully engaging France's army, while the British navy was steadily cutting the lifeline of Canada and the mother country. In India and Africa, British troops were seizing French trading posts. Pitt remained more determined than ever to limit the discretion of his commander in chief in America and plan the next campaign entirely himself. Obsessed by his goal of conquering Canada, he did not hesitate to plunge Britain more deeply into debt. Early in December, 1758, he called on the American governors again to support the war and sought from the northern colonies at least twenty thousand men, paid, armed, and provisioned from London, for an offensive against Canada. Then on December 28 he wrote a long letter to Amherst outlining the campaign for 1759:

Wolfe, who had gone home after distinguishing himself at Louisbourg, was to return to America early in the year with twelve thousand troops and a co-operating fleet "to make an attack upon Quebeck, by the River St. Lawrence." This was to be an independent command, with Wolfe promoted to temporary major general. Amherst himself was to "concert the properest Measures" for "an Invasion of Canada" by "way of Crown Point or La Galette or both." The demolished fort at Oswego must be re-established, and "it were much to be wished" that some attack against Fort Niagara could be mounted. Pitt did not yet know of the fall of Fort Duquesne, but he hoped that Forbes or his successor would be utilized in an offensive operation along the frontiers of the southern colonies. Details of raising and supplying the provincials, building ships on the lakes, sending Rangers, carpenters, and cannon to Louisbourg for Wolfe, etc., were added. Everything was to be in readiness to open the extended campaign by May 1, to coincide with Wolfe's stroke. Since it was now March, Amherst must have swallowed a few times as he read the letter.

Response of the colonies to Pitt's request was about what it had been earlier. The northern colonies, anxious to remove the French menace forever, mostly furnished their quotas. In the South, only Virginia showed an effort to comply, but she kept only one regiment in service instead of the two furnished in 1758. Colonel Washington having resigned his Virginia commission in December (he had been elected to the Virginia House of Burgesses and had married a widow with two children), the command was offered to the other colonel, William Byrd, who accepted.

Amherst promptly appointed Brigadier General John Stanwix to replace Forbes and told him to consolidate the British victory in the West. The situation was still precarious. De Ligneris was mustering strength at Venango in order to seize his old location once more. Indians down the Ohio and in the western Great Lakes promised to help him. Militia from Illinois were returning in the spring bringing more Indians. Governor Vaudreuil ordered the commandant at Niagara to send troops down to Venango for De Ligneris to use.

Small war parties jabbed the English late in the spring: St. Blin, with a force of French and Indians, ambushed a wagon train near Fort Ligonier and killed or captured forty. Another party on July 6 tried to take the fort but was driven off by cannon. Meanwhile, a power drive was building up at Venango —seven hundred Frenchmen, seven hundred and fifty Indians, and more coming. At a great council on July 12, De Ligneris called upon the various tribes to be ready to go south with him next morning. Before he had finished speaking, messengers from Fort Niagara handed him a note from Captain François Pouchot asking for immediate reinforcements because he was about to be attacked by a formidable British force. Thus the garrison at rechristened Fort Pitt escaped attack and, in safety, set about their work of completing a new, pentagon fort. Pennsylvania merchants opened a brisk trade with the Indians, as the Ohio Company of Virginia once had hoped to do.

NIAGARA

The expedition against Fort Niagara had grown easily out of two other developments. Troops had been set in motion under Brigadier General John Prideaux in May, 1759, ostensibly to rebuild the fort at Oswego, as ordered by Pitt. Three thousand regulars reached Oswego on June 27, where they were joined by Sir William Johnson and a thousand Iroquois. Thus it was possible to keep the true destination secret under cover of the building operation. The second factor was the willingness of the Iroquois to assist, a reversal of their neutrality discovered by Johnson. British victories in the latter half of 1758 undermined their faith in French arms, and if the redcoats were going to win they wanted to be on the winning side. More particularly, Niagara in English hands might cut off furs from the French lakes and restore some of that trade to the Iroquois.

Thus it was that on June 30 two thousand of the troops and all the Indians took to the waters of Lake Ontario, rowed quickly toward Fort Niagara, and landed three miles east of it on July 4. Left at Oswego were a thousand troops for construction work under Lieutenant Colonel Frederick Haldimand of the Sixtieth, another competent Swiss officer who would rise to distinction later as a governor of Canada.

Captain Pouchot was stunned by the appearance of the enemy, but Fort Niagara was strongly built. Situated on the point of land where the river empties into Lake Ontario, it was protected on the third side by a stone wall and a ditch. Inside the triangle were several wooden structures and a long, three-story stone headquarters building. The garrison amounted to more than six hundred plus some friendly Indians. Pouchot sent off his plea for help to Venango and also warned the commandant of the dependent post at the top of the falls.

Prideaux began digging a zigzag parallel toward the fort with bays for cannon. Another battery was erected on the point of land across the Niagara River. By July 17 heavy cannon and brisk musket fire were destroying the fort and preventing repairs or much retaliation. Unknown to the French, Prideaux was accidentally killed on the nineteenth by a carelessly fired coehorn. Johnson assumed the command. His Indians had already held council with the Senecas who were supporting the French. The Iroquois were not happy about this division in their league. The Senecas in the fort obtained Pouchot's permission to leave and moved up to the falls. The Anglophile

Indians then declared they were going to be neutral and moved off a few miles southward.

The steady pounding by the British not only was breaking open the fort, it was exhausting the defenders. Then on July 23, Pouchot heard from De Ligneris, who had met Captain Charles Philippe Aubry, commandant in Illinois, on Lake Erie. Relief was coming! Six hundred Frenchmen and a thousand western Indians were entering Niagara River. Pouchot got off a reply that they could approach on the west bank and gain the fort, or come down the east side and fall on a British encampment. The two Frenchmen decided on the latter course —even though their Indians deserted them in hordes when they learned they might face the Iroquois. This withdrawal, however, left Johnson's Iroquois feeling free to attack the French.

Lieutenant Colonel Eyre Massy, commanding six hundred troops and six hundred uncertain Iroquois, awaited the French relief column on July 25 behind a barrier of fallen trees on either side of the narrow portage road. The overconfident French approached on a run, shouting and shooting. The British did not reply until the enemy came almost between them. Then on Massy's orders they poured seven rounds into the astonished French. While the enemy wavered, the redcoats leaped over their breastworks and charged closer. The French withdrawal turned into a rapid retreat. Now the Indians raised their war whoop and joined the bloody chase. It ran for five miles, and the Indians spared no one they could reach with tomahawk or knife. Massy had difficulty protecting about a hundred prisoners, which included Aubry, the mortally wounded De Ligneris, and fifteen other officers.

Captain Pouchot was able to see the beginning of the fight,

and at length he learned of its overwhelming outcome. Before sundown he surrendered. The French remembered Fort William Henry and were apprehensive. It is to Johnson's credit that the French garrison was not molested by the Iroquois.

Forts Presque Île and Venango were left isolated and had to be abandoned. The French advance of 1754 had now been wiped out, and the traditional French forts at either end of Lake Ontario were lost. New France was shrinking in size.

As soon as Amherst heard of Prideaux's death, he dispatched Brigadier General Thomas Gage to succeed him. Arriving at Oswego in the middle of August, Gage found Johnson there with his victorious troops and prisoners, minus a garrison left at Fort Niagara. Gage spurred the work of reconstructing the Oswego fort. His second duty, mentioned in Pitt's letter to Amherst, was to move down the St. Lawrence sixty miles and seize La Galette (Ogdensburg, New York). He learned, however, that Lévis was there with eighteen hundred troops. He also figured that only a thousand redcoats could be spared from fort-building for such an expedition. It was clear to Gage that the objective could not be reached, and he so notified Amherst on September 11. The commander in chief was not happy over this decision.

At the same time, Amherst himself had accomplished little. Having gathered seven thousand men by the middle of June —not Pitt's target date of May 1—he had moved fifteen miles from Fort Edward to Lake George and there spent a month laying out a new fort. Finally, on July 21 he advanced down the lake toward Ticonderoga. On landing he began dragging his cannon along, as Abercromby had failed to do. The advancing troops were met by enemy cannon fire that held them up four days, until the heaviest artillery was eased into position ready to blast the stone fort.

Little did Amherst know that only four hundred Frenchmen, under Captain d'Hébercourt, held the fort. Brigadier General Bourlamaque and twenty-five hundred troops had fallen back toward Fort St. Frédéric. Montcalm's instructions to give way were based on an inner ring of defense: La Galette on the west, Île-aux-Noix in the Richelieu River on the south, Quebec on the east. Lake Champlain would not be disputed. On the night of July 26, therefore, Captain d'Hébercourt blew up the mined fort and joined his commander at Fort St. Frédéric. The ruined Ticonderoga was a gift to Amherst. On the last day of the month Bourlamaque ordered Fort St. Frédéric blown up too, and he retired down the lake to the new fort then under construction on Île-aux-Noix. Amherst settled down for two months of rebuilding the forts at Ticonderoga and Crown Point, when one would have been enough. Invasion of Canada was postponed, and in October it was abandoned.

QUEBEC

Only one of Pitt's contemplated three prongs was left to stab Canada. That was the direct assault on Quebec by water. For several weeks it appeared that this prong too might be blunted.

Wolfe had set out from England with his naval counterpart, Vice Admiral Charles Saunders, on February 14, 1759. They reached Halifax on April 30 and because of ice floes could not get into Louisbourg harbor for two more weeks. Troops were arriving, but not the promised twelve thousand. When Wolfe and Saunders embarked again early in June for Quebec, they carried fewer than nine thousand regulars and four hundred

Rangers. If Wolfe was disappointed in his strength, he admired most of his fellow officers. Robert Monckton, thirty-three, his second in command, was experienced from fighting in Nova Scotia and would be named governor of New York. Aristocratic George Townshend, thirty-five, the second brigadier, was not impressed by Wolfe and was not Wolfe's choice; he was later the unpopular lord lieutenant of Ireland. Ambitious James Murray, thirty-eight, the junior brigadier, became governor of Canada after the war. The senior staff officers were Colonel Isaac Barré, deputy adjutant general and later to sit in Parliament, and Colonel Guy Carleton, deputy quartermaster general and another future general and governor of Canada. In veteran Ralph Burton and William Howe (the third of the Howe brothers in the American theater) he had at least two able battalion commanders. Over-all it was an impressive team. The naval rear admirals were Philip Durrell and Charles Holmes, whose co-operation was exceeded only by their competence, and several ship captains were later to become famous.

Proceeding slowly up the St. Lawrence, the huge squadron of forty-nine naval warships and one hundred and nineteen transports and supply vessels came to anchor on the south side of Île d'Orleans on June 27, without the loss of a single ship. They were not more than five miles from Quebec. The upper town rose proudly on its rocky eminence two hundred feet above the St. Lawrence. A lower town nestled on a ledge close to the water under the shadow of the great bluff. On the north side the St. Charles River flowed southeasterly into the St. Lawrence, pocketing the city in a V. Only the west side lay open, and old Governor Frontenac had begun fortifying it in 1693 by an earthwork running north and south between the two rivers. The French engineer De Lery strengthened the line in 1720, but it was the capture of Louisbourg in 1745 that shocked the governor and De Lery into resuming work on a new wall. Unfortunately the wall was built first, and then the traditional ditch or dry moat in front of it could not be made deep enough, because the rocky subsoil required blasting, and blasting would damage the wall. By 1749 Quebec was enclosed by a barrier running north from Cape Diamond, a spot 350 feet above the St. Lawrence; consequently the wall ran down hill to the St. Charles. Moreover, the cannon were placed to fire north and south along the wall to prevent scaling; they could not fire westward across the Plains of Abraham. French officers considered the west side weak.

So did Wolfe. His first problem was how to get up on the plains on the west side. Should he go ashore below the mouth of the St. Charles and swing around the north side of town, or land far up the St. Lawrence and march down? Inasmuch as the bluff rose high on the north side of the river for several miles above Quebec, Montcalm felt safe from an enemy landing there. Besides, he was convinced that no English ship could pass above Quebec. It was almost an article of faith with him that Wolfe would try to force a landing somewhere down river, between Quebec and the mouth of the Montmorenci River. Therefore he fortified the river's north bank for six miles east of Quebec, made Beauport his headquarters, and waited.

The night after the English fleet came to anchor, the French launched their secret defense weapon: seven blazing ships aimed to set fire to the enemy squadron. All of them failed in their aim, or were hooked by the English and pulled off course. Reputedly this useless effort cost a million livres. On June 30 Monckton landed at Point Lévis on the south shore and moved around to a position opposite Quebec and less than half a mile away. Immediately he began digging in his cannon, ultimately having twenty-nine with which to pound the city.

Unable to penetrate the guarded north shore, Wolfe finally led most of his army ashore on the far side of the Montmorenci River. He met no resistance, for the French would not come out of their entrenchments to fight. Then he made and canceled two plans for assault on those lines. A reconnaissance up the Montmorenci cost him forty-five killed and wounded. The French tried fire rafts again, and again were unsuccessful. Rather desperately Wolfe ordered an attack July 31 on a shore redoubt. Troops from Île d'Orleans were to be run in and joined by Townshend's brigade wading around the mouth of the Montmorenci. The landing boats struck a shoal, but the advance waded ashore and overran the redoubt late in the afternoon. But the English could not advance up the slope to the trenches. Wolfe turned Townshend's men back before a cyclonic rainstorm ended the battle, and the attack was withdrawn. The English suffered two hundred and ten killed and two hundred and thirty wounded, as against sixty casualties for the French. Governor Vaudreuil thought the enemy offensive was finished, but Montcalm declared it to be a prelude.

Wolfe suffered loss of face among his brigadiers, who had not liked his battle plan anyway. A quarrel developed. Casting about for something destructive to do, Wolfe sent Murray up river above Quebec to raid French shipping. He learned that Fort Niagara had fallen. Montcalm, uneasy that English ships had stolen up the river, relied on Colonel Bougainville, who commanded three thousand men with which to prevent Murray from gaining a foothold. Montcalm felt obliged to transfer Brigadier de Lévis with eight hundred men to La Galette to stop the English descent of the river.

The Rangers brought by Wolfe were employed in burning towns down the river and also up the river on the south side. Ultimately the English destroyed more than fourteen hundred houses. Townshend was contemptuous of this kind of warfare. Then Wolfe went down with fever on August 19. Sick, lonely, and discouraged, he finally asked his brigadiers on August 27 to submit their own plan for taking Quebec.

The three officers gathered with Admiral Saunders and in three days drew up a proposal and plan of operations. They insisted that the army be brought together to act as a unit, and that a landing be made above Quebec, twelve to seventeen miles west of the city, which at least would put the army across the line of French supplies coming from farther up the river. Wolfe assented, and the concentration began. On September 1 and 2 the troops at Montmorenci were withdrawn to Île d'Orléans, then landed on Point Lévis. Five hundred were left at the west end of the island under Carleton, and sixteen hundred were absent raiding down-river habitations under Major George Scott. Another five hundred were posted at Point Lévis under Burton, and thirty-five hundred were crowded on ships for the journey upstream.

Landing on the north shore was scheduled for September 9, but rain postponed the venture. Then Wolfe, cruising down the river, spotted a new landing place much closer to Quebec in a cove called Anse au Foulon. It had a blockaded roadway running diagonally upward to the top of the bluff. Wolfe showed it to his principal officers on the tenth. This was at least his eighth plan of action. The night of September 12 was set for the attempt.

Montcalm was not going to be fooled by the shifting of the enemy forces. "M. Wolf is just the man to double back," he declared, still in expectation of a sudden assault on Beauport, where he remained. He did pull back two thousand men stationed between Beauport and Montmorenci River. Counting fifteen hundred sailors, he had almost fourteen thousand men strung along the river: militia young and old, Canadian regulars, and only twenty-five hundred professionals from France. But although his force outnumbered Wolfe's, the English troops he would meet were all regulars. Montcalm was now fighting for time, because by October the English ships would have to leave the river. The provisions from France were now exhausted, however, and the troops at Quebec were living on the new harvest of the Montreal area. Every few nights provisions boats floated down the river close to the north shore. A convoy was scheduled for the night of September 12, then canceled. For some reason Bougainville did not notify the river posts under his command of the cancellation, a fatal omission.

As a feint, Wolfe ordered small boats assembled to pick up the thousand men under Burton and Carleton and row toward Beauport, to keep Montcalm's attention. Then at two o'clock in the morning boats left the English ships far up the river and rode silently with the current and the ebb tide toward Anse au Foulon, since known as Wolfe's Cove. They carried the first wave of eighteen hundred men. They were to be followed later by the ships containing another seventeen hundred, whose landing operation was commanded by Admiral Holmes.

In the first boats sat Lieutenant Colonel Howe and two hundred light infantry and General Wolfe. The lead boat held twenty-four volunteers under Captain William Delaune of Wolfe's regiment, the Sixty-seventh. The dark flotilla was challenged four times from the shore, but a French-speaking Captain Fraser answered "La France" and "Vive le roi." The sentinels

The Taking of Quebec, 1759. (Clements Library, University of Michigan.)

assumed they were the provisions boats and ran along the shore crying, "Laissez les passer!"

The lead boats went a little too far before grounding at four o'clock. Delaune took his platoon back to the path to clear it of a blockade. Howe ordered his men to scale the 175-foot cliff in front of them, and up they crawled, hanging on to undergrowth. Wolfe climbed with them. On top of the cliff was a picket of a hundred men under Captain Louis de Vergor, who had been surprised at Fort Beauséjour in 1755. Surprised again, he put up resistance until wounded, and half his men were captured. But he had time to dispatch a messenger into the city, and the musket fire was heard though misinterpreted.

The slanting path was now opened, and all the troops went puffing up. The second wave came in from the ships now anchored in midstream. Then the men under Burton and Carleton left the Beauport area and made for the cove. All the forty-five hundred British troops were up on the Plains of Abraham by eight o'clock. Even two cannon were dragged up. The landing, moving without a hitch, was "a professional triumph."[1]

French blunders multiplied. Quebec signaled to Beauport that something important had happened but did not send an explanatory message to Montcalm. Vergor's messenger ran into camp just east of the St. Charles River bridge but nobody believed him. Governor Vaudreuil was told at six o'clock of a British landing—which must have been repulsed, it was added, because musket fire had ceased! He wrote to Bougainville, but

---

[1] This is Colonel Stacey's expression in *Quebec, 1759.* Not all of Wolfe's troops, more than nine thousand, can be accounted for at this moment. The forty-five hundred before Quebec and the sixteen hundred downstream under Major Scott amount to only sixty-one hundred. Wolfe had suffered four hundred and forty casualties at Montmorenci. Some men, apparently of the artillery, were still left at Point Lévis and Ile d'Orleans; others certainly were sick.

did not order him down to Quebec. When Montcalm did ride to the city after daylight, he was shocked to see a long, double, scarlet line on the Plains of Abraham. Deciding then to form and attack without waiting for Bougainville to come up behind the British, he gathered forty-five hundred men, half of them regulars, by ten o'clock and ordered them forward, drums beating and banners held high. Meanwhile his militia had been skirmishing with either end of the British line.

The French advance was impetuous and irregular. They fired too soon, while out of range, then came on raggedly. Wolfe had forbidden any firing until the French came within a deadly sixty yards. Then the platoons began firing in succession. The French advance halted. More or less in unison the British delivered a general volley. The French turned and ran.

Wolfe was hit three times, and four officers gathered around him on the ground. Hearing that the enemy was in flight, he issued a final order, then turned on his side and added, "Now, God be praised, I will die in peace." Monckton was wounded in the lungs, and Carleton and Barré were hit. Townshend assumed command.

Montcalm, too, was mortally wounded in the retreat and had to be held in his saddle until he got into the city. He was carried into a house and died early the next morning. His two senior officers were also killed. Bougainville finally came in view of the battlefield, but Townshend frightened him off. This change of front allowed Montcalm's survivors to escape across the St. Charles and reach the Beauport camp, where Governor Vaudreuil took charge. According to Vaudreuil the French force suffered six hundred and forty-four casualties, but double that number has also been counted. The British lost fifty-eight killed and six hundred wounded.

That night the French marched up the far side of the St. Charles and joined Bougainville's force to the west of Quebec. Vaudreuil sent for Lévis to command the army and told the commandant of Quebec, De Ramezay, to surrender when his food ran out.

The British began deliberate siege operations against the city. As it was already short of food, De Ramezay surrendered on September 17, the very day Lévis reached camp and hoped to relieve the city. The Quebec garrison was transported to France, but the property and persons of the inhabitants were respected. Monckton went to New York for medical attention, and Townshend set out for England. Saunders provisioned the city and then sailed away on October 18. Brigadier General Murray was left as governor of Quebec, standing between a disheartened and hungry French army and hope of relief from France.

The capture of Quebec had been almost too big an assignment for Wolfe. Had he been stubborn he might have crippled his army in a fruitless attack. But he showed he could learn and change his mind (perhaps too often) and in the end he agreed to the plan of his brigadiers, altering it only at the last moment to insist on a new landing place that was luckily seized. As a result, he vindicated Pitt's choice and died a hero. Montcalm handled his position with greater skill, but after Bougainville's failure to protect his shore, he too quickly entered the battle he had so long avoided, risking everything for complete victory or complete defeat.

ST. FRANCIS

One final episode in 1759 aroused a double celebration in the northern colonies. Aware that his timetable was badly disrupted, Amherst took the conservative course at Lake Champlain. His only offensive move after August 1 was to dispatch Major Robert Rogers and two hundred Rangers to rub out an old sore spot, the Christian Indian town of St. Francis on the river of the same name near its confluence with the St. Lawrence (modern Odanak, near Pierreville, Quebec), about fifty miles below Montreal. This nest had bred numerous bloody forays into New England and New York for years, but Amherst's ire had been aroused principally because those Indians had captured two of his officers on their way to make contact with Wolfe.

On the same day as the battle on the Plains of Abraham, Rogers set out down the lake, circled the French at Île-aux-Noix, and cut northeastward to the St. Francis River. Because of illness, injuries, and a gunpowder explosion, he had to send back a quarter of his men. He came in sight of the Indian town on October 2 and observed a night of revelry in progress. In the following gray dawn the Rangers struck the sleeping town in vengeful slaughter. Warriors were shot or stabbed on sight, and torches were laid to every hut. When the terrorized savages bolted for the river, a hidden detachment of Rangers rose and mowed them down. After the holocaust only the Jesuit priest and a score of squaws and children remained. Five female white captives were recovered. Rogers reported seeing "about 600 scalps, mostly English" and therefore did not regret that "we had killed at least two hundred Indians." But others had got away or were not at home that night, and Rogers knew he would be pursued. His men filled their bags with corn and started south toward Lake Memphremagog and the Connecticut River. They broke up into small parties to confuse their trackers. Food gave out, but Rogers had arranged for supplies to meet them at the Wells River junction with the Connecticut. The relief failed him, and the starving men rafted themselves fifty miles down to Fort Number 4. Rogers stayed there, sending rescuers north to find the wandering parties. He had lost only one man at St. Francis, but forty-nine were overtaken in the desperate flight southward. New England rejoiced as much over the fall of the savage capital as she did over the capture of Quebec. Families on the northern frontier felt they could now sleep peacefully at night.

Important as were these victories in North America in 1759, it was a year of English triumphs in other theaters of war, too. There were conquests of French posts in India, the capture of Guadeloupe in the West Indies, defeat of the French army at Minden, Germany, and the gradual immobilization of the French fleet. Repeated naval engagements culminated in the decisive battle of Quiberon Bay, below Brest, on November 20, where Admiral Sir Edward Hawke nipped a contemplated invasion of Scotland and shattered France's naval strength.

X

Victory Removes an Antagonist

The year 1759 had been one of unrelieved disaster for New France. Winter suspended military operations, with two British forces poised for descent on Montreal, the new capital. There could be no escape from impending doom, General Lévis knew, without early and substantial aid from France. He asked for troops, for cannon, and for provisions.

But Louis XV and his ministers had an army at home to maintain, and a blockade by Britain's navy that left France unable to succor her colonies. Canada had never been able to support herself, even in time of peace, and now was more dependent than ever. Was it worth saving, harried ministers asked? Where were more regiments to be found? Would a convoy escape British capture? And something must be wrong with the distribution of supplies already sent and the enormous amounts purchased for the military in Canada. The pungent smell of corruption had been wafted to France, but the culprits were not yet identified. Feebly the court gathered only four hundred recruits and a little more food and sent them off —only to be captured by the British navy.

Plucky Lévis had not waited. In April, 1760, he activated his mixed army of seven thousand men and boldly pushed down the river toward Quebec. He had recalled Bourlamaque from Île-aux-Noix and sent the less reliable Bougainville there.

Murray had a garrison of less than thirty-nine hundred, but he went out on April 28 to meet the enemy on the high ground Montcalm had occupied. He also had a field artillery of twenty-seven guns. The position he took was sound, but he did not keep it. When he saw Lévis' advance start to dig in, Murray ordered a quick attack in the snow before the main body should come up. He was briefly successful, but the French columns did come up and hammered on his flanks until the tide turned. The red line broke and the British fell back into the city, losing all but two of their cannon. It was a bloodier engagement than Wolfe's, for the British lost two hundred and fifty-nine killed and eight hundred and forty-five wounded. Lévis lost one hundred and ninety-three killed and six hundred and forty wounded, including the active Bourlamaque, in what is usually called the Battle of Ste. Foy. He now laid siege to Quebec, and if French ships had arrived, Murray might have had to capitulate. But on May 15 British ships appeared and immediately shot up the frigates that were supporting Lévis. The Frenchman saw that the jig was up and pulled back to Montreal again.

Now it was a matter of time. Amherst shifted his weight for the 1760 campaign. He sent two regiments from Louisbourg to strengthen Murray at Quebec so that he might move up the St. Lawrence. He reduced his force at Lake Champlain to thirty-four hundred—two regiments of regulars, the four New York Independent Companies, and the New England provincials —and gave over the command to Colonel William Haviland of the Twenty-seventh. They were to push down the lake toward Montreal starting August 10. Amherst himself added his remaining troops to those of Gage at Fort Oswego and took command of the descent of the St. Lawrence with the main army of ten thousand, also starting on August 10. With him were six hundred Iroquois under Sir William Johnson, a distinct achievement because Governor Vaudreuil had earlier sent French-allied Indians to persuade the Iroquois to remain neutral.

To meet this triple threat Lévis did what he could. He had ordered Captain Pouchot, recent commandant of Fort Niagara, to Fort La Galette to hold the upper St. Lawrence. Pouchot selected a nearby island and hurried construction of a fort in midstream—Fort Lévis. He tried to enlist the neighboring Indians but they hung off. The Iroquois succeeded in talking them into remaining neutral. Pouchot was left with only three hundred men and one ship to stem the invasion.

At Île-aux-Noix Bougainville had eleven hundred men. Lévis asked him to hold out as long as possible, but Vaudreuil, interfering as usual, advised him that in the face of a superior enemy he would have to retreat or surrender. Roughly halfway between Montreal and Quebec, Lévis stationed Major Jean Dumas, who had routed Braddock, at Trois Rivières in the hope that the garrison there might slow Murray's advance.

The co-ordinated British offensive moved relentlessly. Haviland swept down Lake Champlain and landed near Île-aux-Noix. Batteries were erected and began pounding the French fort while a detachment swung around it to the Richelieu River below. With only a day's provisions left, Bougainville stole away at night, leaving forty men to surrender on August 28. He hastened northward, burning St. Jean as he passed, to add his troops to the defense of Montreal.

Amherst approached Fort Lévis with numerous row galleys, whale boats, and bateaux. Near the island he put detachments ashore on either side of the St. Lawrence. Pouchot's warship gave a good account of itself before it was captured, and Fort Lévis was reduced to "a litter of carpenter's wood" when Pouchot surrendered on August 25. The British rechristened the stronghold Fort William Augustus and left a garrison to rebuild it. On August 31 the army began descending the dangerous seven great rapids. Although no enemy appeared to harass them, Amherst lost fifty-four boats and eighty-four men in the rocky, turbulent passage.

Meanwhile, Murray had embarked from Quebec with twenty-two hundred men on July 15, expecting to reach Montreal first and seize it alone. His ambition rather exceeded his competence. The journey was constantly against the current, and the wind was unreliable. Passage was slow, and at each parish he sent men ashore to receive the submission of the Canadians, collect their arms, and administer the oath of neutrality on penalty of burning their houses. Near Trois Rivières he paused, then passed it on the far side. Helpless Dumas could only retire upstream just ahead of him. Lévis did not deceive himself: "We possess no means of stopping them; we are making a mere defensive demonstration to retard their march." Murray reached Varenne, just below Montreal, on August 31 and stopped a week waiting for Haviland to join him from the south. Amherst landed on the western end of the island of Montreal on September 6. The timing was perfect.

The Canadians, who had been falling away from Lévis, now

left him completely. Only the battalions of regulars were left to defend the city. Governor Vaudreuil summoned the principal officers and Intendant Bigot on the night of September 6 to discuss capitulation in the face of such overwhelming strength. Bougainville called on Amherst next morning regarding a truce. The general was adamant: he had come to take Canada and would settle for nothing short of it. Proposals were made and argued. Agreement was reached on September 8 in a long treaty providing for surrender of the troops as prisoners, for protection of trading interests and the Catholic Church, and for security of private property. Lévis, failing in his demand for the honors of war, urged Vaudreuil not to sign, but the governor saw that Amherst's terms were generous and gave up the whole of Canada. In a final defiance, Lévis burned his battalion flags and declared they had been destroyed earlier.

Amherst had won for his king a domain twelve times the size of England. Canada was actually of unknown extent. The Hudson Bay posts were now contiguous to New England. Westward the province stretched through the Great Lakes to boundaries undetermined; it angled southward to include the Ohio Valley and the vague Illinois country. The very next day after the capitulation General Amherst detached the redoubtable young Ranger commander, Major Robert Rogers, with two of his companies to row up the St. Lawrence and the lakes to take over the western posts and raise the British flag.

On his way Rogers reported to Brigadier General Monckton at Fort Pitt and picked up Johnson's deputy Indian agent, George Croghan, and a company of the Sixtieth Regiment to garrison Detroit. The Indians of the Detroit River looked forward to the new "tenants" of the fort, as they considered them, anticipating gifts and supplies from the victorious power. On

Victory Removes an Antagonist

November 29, 1760, in appropriate ceremonies, Rogers marched into Fort Detroit and raised his flag, while the small French garrison under Captain Bellestre marched off to Fort Pitt under guard as prisoners of war. Rogers then sent two squads of Rangers to the southwest to occupy Fort Miamis (Fort Wayne, Indiana) and Fort Ouiatenon (near Lafayette, Indiana). He himself attempted to lead a party up the lakes to Fort Michilimackinac (Mackinaw City, Michigan) but was turned back by ice. That fort as well as one on Green Bay and another at modern Niles, Michigan, would have to wait until the next summer. Croghan held a series of Indian conferences and promised a trade at fair prices. He also obtained the release of fifty-seven white captives. They went back east with the Rangers late in December.

To establish a makeshift government for Canada, Amherst divided the province into three districts. Murray was continued as military governor of the Quebec or eastern district. Burton was named military governor of the Trois Rivières region, and Gage was appointed military governor of the Montreal district. Militia captains were given powers as justices of the peace to settle local disputes. Provisions were distributed, and trade goods called for from American merchants. Life for the Canadian habitant moved along much as it had before, pending a general treaty of peace by which he assumed Canada would be restored to France once more.

THE CHEROKEE REVOLT

Yet the fighting was not ended, and a formal treaty was more than two years away. One trouble spot was the back country of the Carolinas, where the Cherokees had taken up the hatchet. Numbering ten thousand distributed in forty towns, they resented four western settlements, on Long Canes Creek and at Ninety-Six in western South Carolina, and two recent forts: Fort Prince George on the Keowee River (Pickens County on the extreme western border of South Carolina) and Fort Loudoun on the Little Tennessee River (near Vonore, Tennessee, thirty-five miles southwest of Knoxville). The latter post, established in 1756, stood near the Cherokee capital of Chota and was the first English fort on the west side of the Appalachians. The neighboring Cherokee women, enjoying great personal freedom, soon were living with many men of the garrison.

The Cherokees were divided into pro-French and pro-English factions. Border killings occurred all spring and summer of 1759. When numerous headmen went to Charleston to try to negotiate peace, they were illegally held as hostages. Governor William Henry Lyttelton ordered the Cherokees deprived of ammunition and led South Carolina militia to Fort Prince George to threaten them in November. Chief Attakullakulla, who had visited England in 1730 and remained steadfastly pro-British, could not deliver up the twenty-five murderers wanted by the governor. The Carolina troops, restless over an advancing wave of smallpox, forced Lyttelton to agree that, as soon as the guilty raiders were brought in, the hostages at Fort Prince George would be released and the presents at the fort (three tons of powder, balls, muskets, and woolens) would be distributed. Lyttelton marched out on December 31 leaving a tinderbox—a smallpox epidemic, sullen Cherokees who would never surrender the guilty ones, resentful relatives of the innocent hostages, and the needed ammunition that could be obtained only by force. Governor Louis de Kerlérec of Louisiana tried to aggravate the Cherokees' hostility but lacked the powder and trade goods to encourage them.

The rebellious members of the tribe tried to take Fort Prince George by trickery in February, 1760, and failed, although they killed the commandant. In revenge the soldiers butchered the hostages. Cherokee war parties killed fifteen traders and forty-six settlers, captured many more, and attacked Ninety-Six. They pushed back the frontier almost a hundred miles. When South Carolina appealed for regulars, Amherst sent two regiments from Pennsylvania under Colonel Archibald Montgomery, with recently exchanged Major James Grant as second in command. The regulars marched to Ninety-Six in May and destroyed five Indian towns, killing sixty to eighty warriors, on their way to Fort Prince George. Since no Indians sued for peace, Montgomery moved along toward Fort Loudoun, a hundred miles northwest. He was attacked and lost seventeen killed and sixty-six wounded while killing about fifty Cherokees. Cautioned by Grant and thinking he had done enough, he did not go on. He left provisions and reinforcements at Prince George and returned to Charleston, where he finally posted four companies. The Cherokees believed the British had retreated in fear of them.

Isolated Fort Loudoun, containing two hundred militia under Captain Paul Demeré, was besieged all spring and summer by Oconostota. South Carolina had asked Virginia to send relief, since the northern route was shorter, and the Virginia Assembly agreed to dispatch the regiment under Colonel William Byrd. He started slowly on the 300-mile journey in July. But by early August the Loudoun garrison was starving and mutinous. Captain Demeré asked the Cherokee chiefs for terms and surrendered on August 8. His troops and their families were to be escorted to Fort Prince George. Early on the second morning out, however, they were attacked by their Cherokee escorts. Demeré was horribly mangled, some thirty-five others were slain, and the survivors divided up as captives. Attakullakulla, who was still for peace, rescued his friend Captain John Stuart, an agent to the Cherokees, and delivered him to Colonel Byrd. The latter sent a blustering message to the Cherokee war leaders but halted his march. Oconostota sought French aid in New Orleans.

South Carolina, its governor called home, appealed again to Amherst for troops, and he sent back a detachment under James Grant, now a lieutenant colonel, that arrived in Charleston in January, 1761. This time the province also raised a regiment and six hundred mounted rangers under such officers as Francis Marion, Dr. William Moultrie, and Henry Laurens. With more than twenty-eight hundred men, Grant reached Fort Prince George in May. It was now commanded by Lieutenant Lachlan McIntosh, whom the Indians respected and who had ransomed one hundred and thirteen white prisoners, including seventy from Fort Loudoun. Oconostota was ready to talk peace, but Charleston wanted vengeance, and Amherst had ordered chastisement for the massacre of the Fort Loudoun garrison. When Grant pressed on, he was attacked on June 10. His losses were small and he carried out a systematic destruction of fifteen Indian towns and their crops. The Cherokees living beyond the demolished Fort Loudoun could see what was in store for them and were ready to have Attakullakulla plead for them. He brought in a few chiefs to Prince George, and terms were dictated by Colonel Grant. Attakullakulla objected to one stipulation and insisted on going to Charleston to see the lieutenant governor. The clause was modified, but the other terms included a boundary line in the west between Indian and white settlements, all white captives to be delivered up, future Indian murderers to be executed by their own chiefs, white murderers to be tried in Charleston, and no Frenchman to be allowed in Cherokee country. The treaty was signed on December 17, 1761, yet its chief effect was to solidify Cherokee hatred of the English.

RECEDING DRUMS

With the fall of Canada, Governor Vaudreuil, Intendant Bigot, the two generals, Colonel Bougainville, Major Péan, other officers and civil officials departed for France. If some of them were bitter over lack of support from Versailles, others may have been uneasy over their coming reception. Loss of Canada had not been viewed kindly by the ministry, and the inevitable attempt to find a scapegoat had inspired re-examination of the support previously given to the province. In the course of this investigation, evidence of flagrant corruption was uncovered. Therefore, upon arrival Vaudreuil, Bigot, and forty others were clapped in the Bastille, accused of fraud and peculation.

Trials for twenty-one of them commenced in December, 1761; like thieves they began to accuse one another, and the whole sordid story came out. Provisions sent for troops had been sold to traders; then supplies purchased in Canada were bought at artificially high prices, as were ships hired for military purposes. Yet farmers were forced to sell their grain first to Bigot at low fixed prices. Gifts to Indians were overpriced. Entertainments had been charged off to the king. With excessive profits accruing to a few, gambling and wenching ran high. Vaudreuil and seven others were acquitted; the governor had not profited, but he certainly could not have been ignorant of the dishonest traffic. Bigot was fined a million and a half livres as restitution, his property was confiscated, and he was banished from France for life. Joseph Cadet, commissary general, was fined six million livres and banished from Paris for nine years. Others were fined and imprisoned. Thirty-four of the accused failed to appear for trial, but seven were sentenced *in absentia.*

The three military commanders were not involved. Lévis became a marshal of France and was eventually created a duke. Bourlamaque and Bougainville continued their military careers, although the latter transferred to the navy, became a noted explorer of the East Indies, and is better remembered for an island in the Solomon group and a tropical flower that were both named for him.

Meanwhile, France had lost her last stronghold in India in April, 1761, and had surrendered the island of Dominica in June. Peace negotiations with England were proposed, but Pitt was suspicious. The French, indeed, were hoping to trade their conquests in Hesse and Göttingen for Canada. Pitt insisted on keeping all the conquered parts of the French empire. Frederick the Great was not satisfied either, but British public opinion was divided over continuing the war for his benefit.

Rebuffed, France listened to a Spanish proposal to form an alliance and dragged Spanish complaints into the discussion. Pitt refused even to consider Spanish issues, and the tentative negotiations broke down. On August 15 the Bourbon Family Compact was secretly signed. King Ferdinand of Spain had wisely remained neutral throughout the war, earning England's gratitude, but after his death in 1759, Charles III, strongly sympathetic to France, succeeded him. He demanded certain concessions from England over ship seizures, logwood in Honduras, and cod in Newfoundland. He thought he could gain his points by an alliance with an already defeated France, but Spain was entering the war too late to reap anything but disaster.

Pitt suspected an alliance and in September asked the cabinet to declare war on Spain. The new king, young George III, wanted peace, not further war, and so did some of his ministers. They had all smarted under Pitt's insolence, bred of success. When Pitt threatened to resign if they did not meet his demand for war, the cabinet dug in its heels and refused to give way. As he had never had a party following, Pitt could bring no pressure on the opposition. So he resigned on October 4, 1761, and was succeeded by the Earl of Egremont. *b [c they wouldn't declare war on fr.]*

A month later the cabinet asked Spain to disavow its suspected alliance with France, and when the Spanish court refused, England declared war, on January 4, 1762. Spain now showed that her first aim was to reconquer Portugal, a neutral friendly to Britain. Her army invaded the poor kingdom in May. In July England sent Lord Loudoun and Brigadier General John Burgoyne with six thousand troops who were able to protect Lisbon until the Spanish forces ignominiously departed. That was only the beginning for Spain. In June an expedition under the Earl of Albemarle, augmented by several regiments from America under Monckton, laid siege to Cuba's El Morro Castle and captured Havana. In October English forces under Brigadier General William Draper and Rear Admiral Samuel Cornish set out from India and took Manila and the Philippines. Such was the fruit of Charles III's foreign policy.

Secret peace talks with France reopened in late spring of 1762. Now that Pitt had left the government, the predatory aims of Frederick had grown more distasteful to England. France had gained nothing from her Spanish alliance. Indeed, France's position had only deteriorated. Bereft of India, all of Canada and half of Louisiana, three of her four West Indies islands, her hopes of holding four so-called neutral islands, and her army driven from Hesse, she had paid heavily for her offensive move into the Ohio Valley. All she had gained was Minorca and two trading posts in Sumatra; she still held two islands in the Indian Ocean. Her fundamental weakness was not that her military and financial commitments in Germany prevented her from strengthening her far-flung colonies, but rather that she lacked trained seamen and essential naval stores for shipbuilding and that she suffered from Britain's blockade and naval superiority.

Spain with much justice had gained nothing and lost Cuba, the Philippines, and part of her navy. She had failed to conquer Portugal or scare the British from Gibraltar. All this in ten months of war was something of a downhill record.

There was not much France could ask as a price for peace. She did put great stress on the return of St. Lucia Island and on fishing rights off Newfoundland. When England indicated acquiescence, ministers were exchanged, and the Duke of Bedford went to Paris in August with detailed instructions. A draft of a treaty was submitted to the cabinet council in October and approved. It was then signed on November 3, 1762, and laid before Parliament.

Canada and all Louisiana east of the Mississippi (except New Orleans) went to England. Free navigation of that river was granted to British subjects. Grenada and three of the neutral islands (St. Vincent, Dominica, and Tobago) remained in British hands. Minorca and the two posts in Sumatra were restored to England. French acquisitions in India made since 1749 were renounced. The fortifications of Dunkerque on the English Channel were to be demolished. French and British armies were to be withdrawn from the German principalities. No compensation was allowed for French ships taken between the outbreak of hostilities in 1754 and the formal declaration of war in 1756.

England conceded fishing rights on the Newfoundland banks to France and returned two small islands in the Gulf of St. Lawrence as fishing stations. Guadeloupe, Martinique, and St. Lucia were restored to France, and she got back the posts in India held before 1749, as well as the slave port of Goree off the west coast of Africa. Canadians were to have the choice of leaving Canada or becoming British citizens.

Spain came out better than she deserved. Although she had to cede Florida to England in order to get back Cuba, it was no great loss; Florida had become an expensive failure. As compensation for the possible loss of Florida, France had promised New Orleans and western Louisiana to Spain; now the pledge had to be redeemed, thereby sweeping France entirely from the mainland of North America and leaving Spain ensconced in a new region. She regained the Philippines because the conquest by England was not known until after the treaty was signed. Spain was denied a share in fishing off Newfoundland, and she was forced to allow British subjects to harvest logwood in Honduras. As for the Spanish ships taken before war was declared, their cases were referred to admiralty courts in England.

An ailing Pitt led the opposition to ratifying this treaty on the grounds that Frederick the Great was not a party to it and that certain conquests were given up. A few voices out-Pitted

The Colonial Wars

Pitt in their objection to any concession to France. Thundered the *North Britain*, under editorship of the rakish John Wilkes, demogogic member of Parliament: "A wicked *faction* only would purchase an *ignoble* and *inglorious peace*, by giving up to the perfidious *French* and to the feeble and insolent *Spaniards* our most valuable and important conquests."

Most such minority criticism was founded on the fame of the West Indies for sugar and on ignorance of the resources of Canada and Florida, both of which were considered by some as largely uninhabitable or not self-sustaining. Frederick, meanwhile, was getting along with peace negotiations on his own with an exhausted Austria.

The Treaty of Paris passed Parliament easily and was formally signed on February 10, 1763. Five days later a separate treaty ended what had come to be a separate war in Germany by a reversion to the status quo ante bellum. Frederick's overweaning ambition had been checked, and it was quietly demonstrated that George III had no further interest in ancestral Hanover and its foreign relations.

REFLECTIONS ON THE PEACE

The Treaty of Paris was a good treaty because, given the circumstances, it was fair. There was a comforting note of finality to it for the British. In truth it ended one chapter of empire history and opened another. Previous treaties by their restoration of too many conquests had simply left old sores to fester. France had lost her American empire as much by ambitions she could not support as by strangling regulations. The tenuousness of legal claims to unoccupied lands based only on exploration stood revealed. France had had her Cartier, Spain her De Soto, and England her Cabots, but charters and assertions written according to who saw what first were no more than vain boasts and challenges. Inevitably it was up to the colonists themselves to make their own boundaries by the drift of their settlements. None of the three powers would recognize a line that the others could not hold by force. The beckoning land had to be won— that is, reclaimed from the wilderness, wrested from the savage, and secured from the rival.

Early in the contest France and England, although professing a desire for peace and knowing that strength was to be gathered only from peace, insisted on a peace that would permit expansion of trade and territory. Each country had developed a sense of mission, whether it was toward the fur trade, saving the souls of the Indians, gaining a new Canaan, wider boundaries, or national prestige. It could not be fulfilled without possession of the interior continent. This was a contradictory or mutually exclusive ambition. One side had to conquer. The irony is that under English rule the French colonials actually achieved more freedom and prosperity than they ever enjoyed under their own government.

The Treaty of Paris elevated Great Britain to the strongest power in Europe with the largest world empire. She had come a long way from her trembling posture before the Spanish armada, her panting rivalry with the Dutch, and her anxiety toward Louis XIV. By the same treaty France passed her zenith and began a gradual decline. Napoleon recovered Louisiana from Spain but did not know enough to keep it. His other conquests were momentary, being chiefly tributes to the egotism that accelerated his country's retrogression. Of more significance, perhaps, France's exit from this continent put the area out of range of the Napoleonic wars to come. North America escaped two decades of exhausting conflict.

The Colonial Wars

Competition between France and England by no means ceased. It persisted for another fifty years. Without hope of regaining her empire, France nevertheless allied herself with the Americans during their revolution to make sure that Britain would likewise lose her extensive possessions on this continent. Successful in this adventure, she then fell victim to the contagion of revolution. The rise of Napoleon again pitted England against her old enemy to stop France from swallowing Europe and the Mediterranean. By 1815 France was thoroughly subdued, and Europe was exhausted. The colonial wars were the first conflicts in this long rivalry and foreshadowed the outcome. They occurred in two pairs of wars that gave ample warning of reforms needed to preserve the French empire—clear to everyone but an absolute monarch.

XI

The Aftermath

For the Anglo-Americans, removal of France as a neighbor ended a source of trouble as old as the colonies. A dream of 1690 had come true, after four long wars; a dream of safety as well as of victory over a rival church. The most immediate change was a feeling of relief on the northern and western frontiers—a feeling not of complete freedom from Indian attack but from combined attacks, from encouragement of savage raids, and from a dangerous rivalry in settlements and land claims. The West lay open, and the Indian stood alone. Spain was too feeble and her territory too distant to serve as the same kind of antagonist. Expulsion of France also checked further development of a dual cultural inheritance in Canada or in the United States. Anglo-Saxon institutions, language, and customs dominated the latter country and came to ascendancy in the former.

The Colonial Wars

The Indians, doomed by the ending of conflict among the colonizing powers, their natural enemies, could no longer count on being courted or placated as allies, even as they could not play one nation against the others. What was worse, they could not even be left alone in the new peace. If it was inevitable that the Americans would expand against their hunting grounds, it was also true that the Indians coveted too many of the white man's goods to sever that contact. Held together by mutual desire, the Indian culture could not survive exposure to the European. Not only did the French lose the war, therefore, but the Indians did too, even those on the side of the English. Their future efforts to preserve their way of life, to strike back, or even to adapt, form a separate and sad story.

The experience of four colonial wars did not disabuse the Anglo-Americans of the adequacy of militia, nor did it render a professional standing army more palatable. The latter was a specific complaint in the Declaration of Independence. Later on in the Constitution, Congress was given power to raise armies and provide a navy, and to organize and arm militia, all to "provide for the common defence." A small regular army (one regiment of infantry and one battalion of artillery) had to be maintained to guard the frontier of federal territory. Two defeats by Indians in the Old Northwest caused this army to be enlarged rather than erased. It was the militia of the states, however, that in national emergencies Congress could call forth to execute the laws, suppress insurrections, and repel invasions. Such calls were to be made through the governors according to state quotas.

Throughout the seventy years of conflict England never solved the primary problem of America's indifference to military service. When the choice was between joining the British regulars or joining the local militia, almost no one would consider the former. Yet the superiority of regulars over militia was repeatedly demonstrated. On occasion the militia performed well —as at Port Royal in 1710, Louisbourg in 1745, and Fort Frontenac in 1758—occasions of talented leadership, short-range objectives, and strong motivation; but for grim campaigning or dull garrison duty, discipline and training told the difference.

When, as a concession, a special regiment of regulars (the Sixtieth) was created for Americans, it had a little appeal, but hardly enough to reach its strength of four thousand. It was still the seasonal militia—with a bounty for joining, the privilege of electing company officers, a short term of duty, a particular objective, and perhaps a grant of land upon discharge— that seemed the least of military evils. Nobody was expected to enjoy army duty, and of course no one in his right mind would enter the British navy. Risk of life was no greater in privateering, where discipline was easier and the chance of rich rewards made the service bearable. The same attitude persisted in the American Revolution and exasperated General Washington. It was the "summer soldier" that drew the sarcasm of Tom Paine. Americans were simply not military minded, and in peacetime abhorred a standing army.

The colonial wars should remind Americans that this country's long policy of isolationism was not traditional from the colonial period. On the contrary! Broad as the Atlantic was to small sailing vessels, the American colonies were quickly embroiled in all European disputes of the seventeenth century and most of those of the eighteenth. When President Washington advised against "entangling alliances" in his Farewell Address, he was not speaking of a condition which the United States had long enjoyed and should desire to perpetuate but of a new ideal it should hope to achieve. It was the political separation from Great Britain, plus the embarrassment of a continuing alliance with a revolutionary France now lapsed into military dictatorship, which inspired the notion that we ought to shun European quarrels over power.

There was some advancement in the art of war during the four wars. They confirmed the doom of fortified cities and most forts. Cannon balls could pulverize all constructions behind an impregnable wall. Further, four operations in the last war—against Louisbourg, Quebec, Havana, and Manila—were amphibious operations that pointed up the necessity of army-navy co-operation. The lesson was easily forgotten, however, and failure in joint undertakings would recur without penalties against the unco-operative commanders.

Weapons changed little: the musket was still basic. Rifled barrels were an improvement over smoothbores, but Europeans were slow to adopt them. However, the tactics of the Rangers, borrowed largely from the Indians and made effective by rifles, doomed the old formations of exposed battle lines firing by platoons. Again, the European armies failed to do more than develop light infantry companies in each regiment for flexibility. The British learned new tactics grudgingly, and Braddock's defeat was repeated by Burgoyne in 1777 and by Pakenham in 1815. It was the unmilitary Americans who in 1775 sought as many rifles as they could get and employed Ranger methods against the "old style" British redcoats.

Subtly perhaps but definitely in this last war the Renaissance made its final conquest of a feudal mind. The internal fault of the French colonial system, like that of Spain, was its medieval cast. France had clung too long to outworn concepts of the Middle Ages. She represented a closed society under four authorities: monarch, church, nobility, and monopoly. She secured obedience and uniformity in New France at the expense of initiative and self-reliance. The dissatisfied at home could not escape by migration. The fur trade was awarded to a company that sent over employees. The Crown rewarded favorites and made sycophants; it dispatched troops and then gave them inducements to remain. The church sent priests and nuns. All these groups were overregulated by appointed officials, military officers, bishops, and company directors. At home the French parlement had no actual governing power and was virtually ignored. No revolution curbed the monarch's power. In New France there was no representative assembly to develop colonial leaders, no competing sects, no critical newspapers, and education was controlled by the church. The variety that makes vitality was missing. The frontier influence could hardly penetrate the insulated colonists.

In Paris, Canada and Louisiana were regarded as parasites on the royal treasury. They ought to return a profit but they did not. Time and again the whole idea of an overseas empire was questioned, because no one understood the prerequisites for successful operation. Only a few individuals, like Champlain or La Salle or Frontenac, who broke from the feudal mold possessed the liberal faith or broad patriotism to envision a French empire of mutually supporting parts. Unfortunately they never had a king with enough imagination to catch their vision, and the measures taken by ministers only exposed the ineptness of a quasi-medieval culture for expansion and variation. It was inelastic and so it cracked under pressure. New France, actually a misnomer, was truly an extension of the Old World, and therein lay its failing.

Parkman has been accused of prejudice in arrogating to the

English several virtues he denied the French, but at least he emphasized that there was a difference in the outlook of the two nationalities in America. The prevailing attitude of most of the French in Canada and Louisiana was grounded on exploitation of the country. The habitants themselves, as well as the trading companies back home, were mercantile in outlook. The purpose of the colony was to make money for promoter and settler. In contrast, a large proportion of the English colonists were antimercantile, not in the sense of being indifferent to making money, but in aiming primarily to establish permanent homes under new governments, to put down roots. In time of war the French colonials fought for their king and church, for their economic opportunities, and then for their own safety; the English fought for their homes and their children's future and then for their king. Certainly they acted as if they had more at stake.

In the period from 1689 to 1762 certain changes took place in the British Empire that were not paralleled in France or Spain. When the first English colonies were founded, England was ruled by the king in council. Parliament, its House of Lords under royal control and its Commons subject to royal pressures, could do no more than trade direct taxes, or subsidies to the Crown, for redress of grievances. There was no department or machinery for administering colonial affairs. They were left to proprietors and commercial companies, who had to make conditions of migration attractive to individual settlers. Failures and difficulties plagued the sponsors, and after many of the colonies had reverted to the Crown, a standing committee of the Privy Council, called the Lords of Trade, was in 1675 put in charge of the colonies. As part of the Glorious Revolution of 1688, Parliament seated new rulers and asserted its constitutional supremacy over the monarchy; then the cabinet system of executive ministers responsible to Parliament, not to the king, began to develop. The Board of Trade became advisory on colonial matters as Parliament consolidated its powers and supervised colonial government. If the British seem modern in contrast to the French and Spanish, the Anglo-Americans were becoming something still different.

The colonies participated in this evolution in their own manner. Assuming that they occupied the same position relative to the Crown as did Parliament, the colonial assemblies proceeded to delimit the powers of royal governors in the same way and to assert increasing authority. They did not recognize any transfer of power over themselves from the Crown to Parliament. Hence, they continued their long struggle for increasing self-government against Parliament for having "arrogated to itself the same absolute power against which it had fought." This spirit of self-dependence, so lacking in Canada and Florida, was on every side encouraged by new developments in colonial life. The immigration of non-English peoples, the wide dispersion of property and participation in government, the growth of emotional religious sects against the established Anglican and Puritan formalism, the decay or denial of safeguards preserving social privilege, the evasion of restrictions on colonial trade, the increasing number of newspapers and colleges, and the vigorous expansion of settlement southward and westward—all were remolding the European emigrant.

The European heritage and native experience were distinctively shaped and colored in English America by the frontier exposure, a subtle transformation which only a few perceptive men could describe. The democratizing influence, the demands on resourcefulness and also co-operation, the repeated experience in self-government, the rich rewards of individual effort, the heady atmosphere of relative freedom, the confidence in the future—all these yeasty factors infused and transformed both immigrants and native-born. They were caught up in the exciting eighteenth-century Enlightenment that emphasized man's potentialities to help himself over the seventeenth-century's view of his depravity and helplessness. The effect might have been fragmented and dissipated had there been no colonial wars to call the colonies together in common effort. The required military exertion against the enemy forced intercolonial co-operation. With each war the colonies found planning together a little easier, and old fears and suspicions and jealousies somewhat allayed. They almost formed a confederation in 1754 to deal with problems on which the British constitution was silent. They uncovered common complaints, forged joint policies, began to recognize the advantages of knocking down barriers, and experienced the joy of united strength. Dimly they perceived that perhaps they ought to work more closely together.

Their greatest discovery by 1762 was not that with help from home they could kick France out of North America but rather that they were a distinct people who were being aided by kinsmen from England. Cousins they might be under a common king, but third- and fourth-generation Americans generally regarded the native Englishman with curiosity and with as much condescension as respect. He was almost a foreigner. They no longer thought of themselves as "transplanted Englishmen"; two-thirds had been born in America and most of the other third was not English anyway. They had become conscious of their separateness whenever they co-operated with British military forces. They had concluded that London society was morally inferior to their own. Their women realized they enjoyed more freedom and legal rights than the women of England or the Continent. Colonial intellectuals were appearing and had formed the American Philosophical Society in 1743. Even the language was different, as both foreigners and Indians had added new words to the vocabulary of the Americans. Already there was an American outlook and an American style of living and acting. This discovery of themselves was the issue of the fourth colonial war. It was a disquieting discovery, and they were as self-conscious as adolescents for a time. "What then is the American, this new man?" asked St. John de Crèvecœur two decades later, and he went on to describe what he saw then as a whole new breed.

In this frame of mind and with the ancient French menace removed, it was inevitable that the Americans would now examine their imperial relations. They had learned about military co-operation and spoken of the political unity necessary for its full accomplishment; they had developed a foreign trade of which they were jealous; they knew what kind of an army suited them, what tactics and weapons seemed most effective, and how to finance war by paper money; they could appeal to everyone through their numerous newspapers; above all they were not awed by regulars or professional officers. Neither meek nor inarticulate, they would define their position and resist coercion. Pressure could only unify them. At the same moment, faced with new and broader problems of an expanded empire and weighted with an immense war debt, Great Britain turned to re-examine her relations with America. For the men in power, her problems proved to be beyond their capacity to solve.

Important Dates

1688	James II driven from English throne; William and Mary made monarchs by Parliament: the "Glorious Revolution"
1689	The War of the League of Augsburg, or King William's War, begins in May
	Iroquois ravage Lachine in July; Governor Frontenac re calls garrisons from Fort Niagara and Fort Frontenac
1690	Schenectady destroyed by French and Indians in February
	Salmon Falls, N.H., attacked in March
	First intercolonial council meets at New York in April
	General Phips takes Port Royal, Acadia, in May
	Casco, Me., attacked in May
	Expedition under Major Winthrop against Montreal fails in August
	Expedition under Phips fails to take Quebec in October
1691	Major Schuyler attacks La Prairie in August
	Major Church marches up the Maine coast in September
1692	York and Wells, Me., attacked by Abenakis and Canadians
	Plymouth and the Maine settlements united to Massachusetts Bay under new charter
	Fort William Henry built at Pemaquid

Important Dates

1693 Mohawks attacked by French and Indians in February

1694 Oyster Bay, N.H., laid waste by Abenakis in July

1696 Fort William Henry captured by French and Indians in July
Onondagas and Oneidas attacked by Governor Frontenac in July

1697 Iberville captures Fort Nelson, Hudson Bay
Haverhill, Mass., raided by Abenakis in March
Treaty of Ryswick, September 30, ends war

1701 Council of eastern and western Indians at Montreal

1702 War of the Spanish Succession, or Queen Anne's War, begins in May
Carolinians under Governor Moore attack St. Augustine in October

1704 Sack of Deerfield, Mass., in February

1707 Pensacola attacked twice by Carolinians
New England expedition under Colonel March fails in two attempts to take Port Royal

1709 Expeditions against Montreal and Quebec fail for want of British support

1710 New England expedition under General Nicholson captures Port Royal in October

1711 Second British-American attempt against Montreal and Quebec fails when British navy gives up
Tuscarora uprising in North Carolina

1713 Tuscaroras crushed by Colonel Moore and neighboring tribes
Treaty of Utrecht, April 11, ends war

1715 Yamasees rise against South Carolina and are forced to flee to Florida

1718 New Orleans founded by Bienville

1724 Norridgewock Abenakis defeated in Maine

1729 Natchez destroy Fort Roselie on the Mississippi

1733 Savannah founded by General Oglethorpe as first settlement in new buffer colony of Georgia

1739 England declares war on Spain in October

1740 Oglethorpe besieges St. Augustine without success

1741 British-American expedition against Cartagena fails

1742 Oglethorpe repulses Spanish attack on Fort Fredericka

1743 Oglethorpe attacks environs of St. Augustine in March

The Colonial Wars

1744　War of the Austrian Succession, or King George's War, begins in March

French capture Canseau, N.S., but fail to take Annapolis Royal

1745　New England expedition under General Pepperrell captures Louisbourg with help of Commodore Warren in June

Saratoga, N.Y., destroyed by French and Indians in November

1748　Treaty of Aix-la-Chapelle, October 18, ends war

1749　Céloron's tour down the Ohio River, burying lead plates of French claim

1754　Colonel Washington and his Virginia militia surrender to French at Fort Necessity in July

Congress of representatives from eight colonies meet at Albany, June and July

1755　Two French forts in Nova Scotia taken by Colonel Monckton in June

General Braddock and his British regulars decisively defeated on banks of Monongahela River in July by French and Indians

Baron Dieskau's French force defeated at Lake George by Generals Johnson and Lyman in September

1756　England declares war on France, May 18, beginning Seven Years' War and continuing French and Indian War

General Loudoun sent to command in America in July

General Montcalm seizes Fort Oswego in August

William Pitt comes to power in England in December

1757　Loudoun fails in attempt against Louisbourg in August

Montcalm takes Fort William Henry in August; Indians kill prisoners

German Flats attacked by French and Indians in November

1758　British attack under General Abercromby on Fort Ticonderoga fails in July

Louisbourg falls to General Amherst in July

Colonel Bradstreet takes Fort Frontenac in August

Fort Duquesne abandoned to General Forbes in November

1759　General Johnson takes Fort Niagara in July

Forts Ticonderoga and Crown Point abandoned to Amherst in July and August

Important Dates

General Wolfe defeats Montcalm and takes Quebec in September

St. Francis destroyed by Rogers' Rangers in October

1760 General Lévis, after winning battle of Ste. Foy, fails to retake Quebec in April

Fort Loudoun, Tenn., surrendered to Cherokees in August

Montreal and all Canada surrender to Amherst in September

1761 Pitt resigns from government in October

Cherokees sign treaty of peace in December

1762 England declares war on Spain in January

Havana falls to British in June

Preliminary treaty of peace signed November 3 in Paris

1763 Treaty of Paris, February 10, ends war

Suggested Reading

The following citations are to a few of the sources used and to the better secondary accounts of the period, where elaboration of certain events may be found. They are taken up roughly in chronological order. Since these are suggestions for additional reading, the several unpublished manuscript collections that were used are not listed.

The most extensive treatment of the colonial wars is found in the seven titles (nine volumes) that Francis Parkman wrote from 1865 to 1892 under the general heading *France and England in North America.* Of course, the series covers much more than the four wars. *Pioneers of France in the New World* (Boston, 1865) is concerned with Champlain and the early settlements to 1635. A better account of Champlain may be found in Morris Bishop, *Champlain, the Life of Fortitude* (New York, 1948). *The Jesuits in North America* (Boston, 1867) continues the pioneer story and French relations with the Indians, Parkman not hesitating to be critical of the priests at times. George T. Hunt, *The Wars of the Iroquois* (Madison, 1940) covers Iroquois conquest of their neighbors in more satisfactory detail. Allen W. Trelease offers a concentrated focus in his authoritative *Indian Affairs in Colonial New*

Suggested Reading

York: The Seventeenth Century (Ithaca, 1960). The first great Indian war has found its best historian in Douglas E. Leach, *Flintlock and Tomahawk: New England in King Philip's War* (New York, 1958).

Parkman's *La Salle and the Discovery of the Great West* (Boston, 1869) covers the seventeenth-century thrust of the French westward and southwestward. The story is carried forward in the *Mississippi Provincial Archives, French Dominion, 1701–1743* (3 vols.; Jackson, 1927–32), edited by Dunbar Rowland and A. G. Sanders, a mine of information on the early history of the Lower Mississippi; and in N. W. Caldwell, *The French in the Mississippi Valley, 1740–1750* (Urbana, 1941). The first two decades of the eighteenth century in Louisiana are also recounted in the Pénicault narrative in *Fleur de Lys and Calumet* (Baton Rouge, 1953), edited by R. B. McWilliams.

The Old Régime in Canada (Boston, 1874) is Parkman's social history of manners and customs in New France under the authority of king, bishop, and trading company. It is an indictment of the feudal tendencies in contrast to the enlightened institutions of England. Defense measures of the colony are better set forth in the first part of *A History of the Military and Naval Forces of Canada* (Ottawa, 1919), published by the historical section of the Canadian General Staff. The standard English work is Sir John Fortescue, *History of the British Army* (London, 1902–20); Volume I is amusing for the author's vehemence against any monarch or act that reduced the strength of the early army.

In *Count Frontenac and New France under Louis XIV* (Boston, 1877) Parkman narrated the actions of King William's War. A more particular approach is to be found in W. J. Eccles, "Frontenac's Military Policies, 1689–1698: A Reassessment," *Canadian Historical Review*, XXXVII (1956), 201–24; and the same author's summary "History of New France According to Francis Parkman," *William and Mary Quarterly*, 3d ser., XVIII (1961), 163–75. For Frontenac's first opponent, see John H. Kennedy, *Thomas Dongan, Governor of New York* (New York, 1930).

Many contemporary reports of the war are found in Volume II of the *Documentary History of the State of New-York* (Albany, 1850), edited by E. B. O'Callaghan. Accounts by individual participants are fairly plentiful. The "Declaration of Sylvanus Davis" is found in the *Massachusetts Historical Collections* (Boston, 1825), 3d ser., I, 101–12. "Winthrop's Journal" is in the *Documents Relative to the Colonial History of New-York* (Albany, 1854), IV, 193–96; "John Schuyler's Journal, 1690" is in the same work, II, 160–62; "Major Peter Schuyler's Journal" is in III, 800–805. Separately published narratives are *A Journal of the Proceedings in the Late Expedition to Port-Royal* (Boston, 1690); Thomas Savage, *An Account of the Late Action of the New-Englanders* (London, 1691); Cotton Mather, *Decennium Luctuosum: An History of Remarkable Occurrences in the Long War* (Boston, 1699). Thomas Church, *Entertaining Passages Relating to King Philip's War* (Boston, 1716) describes also the later military role of Colonel Benjamin Church. Major John Walley's journal of 1690 may be found in Thomas Hutchinson, *History of the Colony and Province of Massachusetts-Bay* (Cambridge, Mass., 1936), Vol. I, edited by L. S. Mayo.

In *A Half-Century of Conflict* (2 vols.; Boston, 1892) Parkman covered Queen Anne's War and King George's War. It is full of exciting detail and generally reliable. Justin Winsor, *Narrative and Critical History of America* (6 vols.; Boston, 1884–89) is an uneven work because of the multiple authorship, but the last two chapters of Volume V take up the struggle in Acadia and Cape Breton and the contest in the St. Lawrence and Ohio valleys. The Deerfield massacre is vividly related in John Williams, *The Redeemed Captive, Returning to Zion* (Boston, 1707). Contemporary accounts of the expeditions against Canada in the first war are found in *The Private Journals Kept by Rev. John* [i.e., Thomas] *Buckingham* (New York, 1825); Jeremiah Dummer, *Letter to a Noble Lord concerning the Late Expedition to Canada* (London, 1712); and Hovenden Walker, *A Journal or Full Account of the Late Expedition to Canada* (London, 1720). These accounts and others were gathered by G. S. Graham into his *The Walker Expedition to Quebec, 1711* (Toronto, 1953). George N. Waller elaborates on the role of Vetch in his biography, *Samuel Vetch, Colonial Enterpriser* (Chapel Hill, 1960), and offers a study of "New York's Role in Queen Anne's War," *New York History*, XXXIII (1952), 42–53. For the interim period a key to the diplomatic shifting of the time is Max Savelle, "The American Balance of Power and European Diplomacy, 1713–1778" in *The Era of the*

Suggested Reading

American Revolution (New York, 1939), edited by R. B. Morris. Lovewell's defeat was a minor incident inflated by publicity in New England rising chiefly from *Lovewell Lamented* (Boston, 1725) by the Reverend Thomas Symmes. The best brief account of the Spanish-English war may be found in Albert Harkness, Jr., "Americanism and Jenkins' Ear," *Mississippi Valley Historical Review*, XXXVII (1950), 61–90.

Parkman's coverage of King George's War was preceded by Samuel G. Drake, *A Particular History of the Five Years French and Indian War, 1744–1749* (Albany, 1870), a bare chronicle with indifferent commentary. Louis E. de Forest brought together ten contemporary accounts in the *Louisbourg Journals, 1745* (New York, 1932), but did not include the anonymous *Lettre d'un Habitant de Louisbourg* (Quebec, 1745), which details the capture of Canseau and the attempt on Annapolis Royal as well.

Contemporary colonial newspapers begin to be of value here, especially the *Boston News-Letter* and the *New York Weekly Journal*. Newspaper coverage of the French and Indian War is much broader and more frequent, of course. Unfortunately, rumors and travelers' reports were trustingly printed and cannot be relied upon without corroborating evidence.

Sometimes considered his finest work, Parkman's *Montcalm and Wolfe* (2 vols.; Boston, 1884) has stood as the classic account of the French and Indian War. He had more sources to draw on, such as: Volume VI of the *Documents Relating to the Colonial History of New-York* (Albany, 1855); William Livingston, *A Review of Military Operations in North America, 1753–1756* (London, 1757); Winthrop Sargent, *The History of an Expedition against Fort Duquesne, in 1755* (Philadelphia, 1855); the defense of Loudoun in *The Conduct of a Noble Commander in America* (London, 1758); *The Conduct of Major Gen. Shirley* (London, 1758); and J. N. Moreau, *Mémoire Contenant le Précis des Faits* (Paris, 1756), which offers the French government's justification for war with England. Two rather contemporary histories of the war of considerable interest are Captain John Knox, *An Historical Journal of the Campaigns in North-America, 1757–1760* (London, 1769) and Thomas Mante, *The History of the Late War in North-America* (London, 1772).

Since Parkman's time, the only study comparable in detail is

The Colonial Wars

Lawrence H. Gipson's first eight volumes covering a broader canvas and limited to the period 1748 to 1763, his *The British Empire before the American Revolution* (New York, 1936–60). It is thorough and well written. New source material became available in two volumes edited by Stanley Pargellis: *Lord Loudoun in North America* (New Haven, 1933) and *Military Affairs in North America* (New York, 1936), taken from the papers of General Abercromby. A. P. James edited the *Writings of General John Forbes* (Menasha, 1938). Ten volumes of *The Papers of Sir William Johnson* (Albany, 1921–51) comprise his correspondence on Indian affairs from 1738 to 1763. J. C. Webster edited the *Journal of Jeffery Amherst, 1758–1763* (Toronto, 1931). The Abbé Casgrain, once critical of Parkman, edited several French journals in *Guerre du Canada, 1755–1760* (Quebec, 1895), *Lettres du Chevalier de Lévis concernant la Guerre du Canada* (Montreal, 1889), and *Lettres du Marquis de Montcalm* (Quebec, 1894). Montcalm's correspondence for the years 1756–58 is translated and published in the *Report of the Public Archives for the Year 1929* (Ottawa, 1930).

Parkman's vivid account of Wolfe's victory on the Plains of Abraham is corrected and clarified by Colonel C. P. Stacey in *Quebec, 1759: The Siege and the Battle* (New York, 1959). Similarly, Stanley Pargellis re-examined "Braddock's Defeat" in *American Historical Review*, XLI (1936), 251–59. Two recent biographies offer new views of the early part of the war: Douglas S. Freeman, *George Washington*, Vol. II (New York, 1948), and John A. Schutz, *William Shirley, King's Governor of Massachusetts* (Chapel Hill, 1961).

A kind of short version of Parkman may be found in Reuben Gold Thwaites, *France in America, 1497–1763* (New York, 1905) in "The American Nation" series. It is an able account but, because of its extensive coverage, treats the first three colonial wars briefly. As for the exploits of Major Rogers there are his own *Journals* (London, 1765) and a new and careful biography by John R. Cuneo, *Robert Rogers of the Rangers* (New York, 1959). From Indian folklore Gordon M. Day has extracted a different version of the St. Francis slaughter in "Rogers' Raid in Indian Tradition," *Historical New Hampshire*, June, 1962.

The Memoirs of Lieut. Henry Timberlake (London, 1765) in-

Suggested Reading

cludes his participation in the Cherokee War, and the introduction by S. C. Williams to the reprint edition (Johnson City, 1927) offers a summary of the war. For a longer study, see David H. Corkran, *The Cherokee Frontier* (Norman, 1962) and the first part of John R. Alden, *John Stuart and the Southern Colonial Frontier* (Ann Arbor, 1944), which also takes up Spanish activity in the French and Indian War.

The weakness of Parkman's study is the inadequate examination of Spain's role in the colonial wars. The lack is somewhat filled by two dissertations: "The Spanish Infantry: The Queen of Battles in Florida, 1671–1702" (M.A. thesis, University of Florida, 1960) by Luis Arana, and "The Governorship of Spanish Florida, 1700–1763" (Ph.D. diss., Duke University, 1959) by John TePaske. The Spanish side of Queen Anne's War is best told in Verner W. Crane, *The Southern Frontier, 1670–1732* (Durham, 1928) and in Charles Arnade, *The Siege of St. Augustine, 1702* (Gainesville, 1959). Volume VII of the *Collections of the Georgia Historical Society* (1909) is also devoted to the siege of St. Augustine. Continuing warfare in the South is the subject of the *Colonial Records of the State of Georgia* (Atlanta, 1904–15), edited by A. D. Candler, the first six volumes and Volumes XXI–XXV. James Oglethorpe is credited with authorship of *An Impartial Account of the Late Expedition* (London, 1742). Charles Arnade has contributed a revealing article in "The Failure of Spanish Florida," *The Americas*, XVI (1960), 271–81. Chapter 4 of Kathryn Abbey, *Florida, Land of Change* (Chapel Hill, 1941) tells something of the Spanish side of rivalry with England.

Index

NOTE: Forts will be found alphabetically under the general heading of "Forts." British Army regiments will be found by number under the heading "British Army." Indians are under tribal names.

Index

Index

The Colonial Wars

Index

Murray, Brig. James, 186; sent above Quebec, 188; governor of Quebec, 193, 201; battle of Ste. Foy, 197; advances to Montreal, 199

Mutiny Act, 22

Narragansett, 20
Natchez (Indians), 81, 85–86
New Orleans, founding of, 81
Newcastle, Duke of, 109–10, 153–54
Nicholson, Gov. Francis, 32, 69–72, 82–83
Nipmuck, 20
Niverville, Ens. Boucher de, 112
Noble, Col. Arthur, 111–12
Noyan, Capt. de, 174

Oconostota, Chief, 204
Oglethorpe, James, 87, 89–96
Ohio Company of Virginia, 122, 126
Ottawa, 18, 59, 145
Oyster Bay, N.H., 47

Palmer, Col. John, 84, 90
Paper currency, colonial, 38, 61
Parkman, Francis, 217
Péan, Capt. Michel, 127–29, 205
Pemaquid, Me., 22, 43, 48
Penobscot, Me., 22, 47, 49–50
Pensacola, 58, 66, 81–82. See also Fort San Carlos
Pepperrell, Sir William, 100; besieges Louisbourg, 103–6; his regiment, 151
Pequot, 19
Périer, Gov., 86
Philip V, 59, 73, 77
Phips, Sir William, 30–31, 36–38, 43, 53
Pickawillany, 126–27
Picquet, Abbé François, 108, 162
Pitt, William, 89; view of the war, 155; estimate of, 160; changes Loudoun's objective, 161; recalls Loudoun, 165; plans for 1758, 166; organizes Louisbourg ex-

pedition, 169; plans for 1759, 179; resigns, 207; opposes treaty, 209
Population of colonies, in 1690, 34; in 1715, 79–80; in 1756, 154; of European powers, 154
Port Royal, 30–31, 64, 66–67, 69–70. See also Annapolis Royal
Portneuf, Capt., 31, 43
Potawatomi, 18, 59, 145
Pouchot, Capt. François, 181; surrenders Fort Niagara, 184; commands La Galette, 198–99
Powhatan Confederation, 18
Prideaux, Brig. Gen. John, at Niagara, 180–81; killed, 181

Quebec, 8, 12, 14, 60; Phips attacks, 30, 33, 36–37; Schuyler sent to, 53; prisoners sent to, 65; attack planned 1709, 69; Walker approaches, 72; ships escape from, 148; captured by Wolfe, 192

Rale, Fr. Sebastien, 84–85
Ramezay, J. R. de, 111, 193
Raystown (Bedford), Pa., 175–76
Rhett, Col. William, 66
Rigaud de Vaudreuil, P. F., 109, 162
Rogers' Rangers: organized, 153; enlarged, 160; attack St. Francis, 194–95; sent to Detroit, 200–201
Rouville, Capt. F. H. de, 30–31, 63, 67–68

Saco, Me., 47, 51, 62
Saint Augustine: founded, 7, 17; Moore attacks, 61; reinforced, 65; 92; Palmer threatens, 84; Oglethorpe threatens, 89; Oglethorpe besieges, 90, 95
St. Castin, Baron de, 22, 31, 43, 49, 64
St. Clair, Sir John, 139, 145, 152, 175
St. Francis, Que., 24; destroyed, 194
St. Julhien, Col. de, 170
St. Pierre, Capt. J. L. de, 131, 150
Ste. Hélène, J. L. de, 28, 37

Index

Washington, George, 130; reaches Fort Le Bœuf, 131; leads militia west, 132; at Fort Necessity, 133–34; reduced, 135; joins Braddock, 140; advice to Braddock, 144; opinion of battle, 147; rank restored, 159; opposes Forbes's route, 175–76; on march, 178; resigns, 180; opinion of militia, 215

Washington, Capt. Lawrence, 92

Webb, Maj. Gen. Daniel, 157–58; to hold New York, 160; at Fort Edward, 162; reputation ruined, 164

Wells, Me., 42, 62

Wentworth, Brig. Gen. Thomas, 91

Westbrook, Col. Thomas, 84–85

Whitmore, Brig. Gen. Edward, 170–72

Wilkes, John, 210

William and Mary, 22, 60

Williams, Col. Ephraim, 149–50

Williams, Eunice, 64

Williams, Rev. John, 63–64

Winthrop, Maj. Fitz-John, 33, 35

Witchcraft in Mass., 45

Wolcott, Col. Roger, 100

Wolfe, James, 169; at Louisbourg, 170; ordered to Quebec, 179, 186; attacks at Montmorenci, 188; sick, 189; defeats Montcalm, 192; killed, 192

Yamasee, 20, 75–76, 84

York, Me., 63

Zuñiga, Gov., 61